T0305898

Brexit and the Future of the European Union

Following the British referendum held on June 23, 2016, voters supported the withdrawal of the UK from the European Union (EU) (Brexit), a starting point for the third round of European crisis, following the eurozone debt crisis and the migration crisis. This volume provides an overview of the process and consequences of Brexit for EU member states, with an emphasis on possible future EU-UK relations, and a particular focus on countries in Central and Eastern Europe (CEE).

The authors assess the extent to which firms in CEE states have already put in place strategies to counter the new economic reality post-Brexit and identify the strategies that firms are exploiting to better cope with the anticipated implications of Brexit. The book includes a ranking of countries most and least likely to be affected by Brexit; identification of the main determinants of the expansion of companies on the British market and the creation of a typology of strategies used by these companies in the face of Brexit. The book stands out as a complex and multidimensional research work that draws its roots from distinct yet simultaneously interlinked research areas.

It will find a broad audience among academics and students across diverse fields of study, as well as practitioners and policy makers. It is a key reference for all those who want to better understand the complex nature of Brexit and its implications, not only for EU member states but, first and foremost, the business environment.

Marian Gorynia is Full Professor at the Poznań University of Economics and Business.

Barbara Jankowska is Full Professor at the Poznań University of Economics and Business.

Katarzyna Mroczek-Dąbrowska is Associate Professor at the Poznań University of Economics and Business.

Routledge Studies in the European Economy

For more information about this series, please visit www.routledge.com/series/SE0431

Brexit and the Future of the European Union

Firm–Level Perspectives

Edited by Marian Gorynia, Barbara Jankowska and Katarzyna Mroczek-Dąbrowska

Routledge
Taylor & Francis Group

LONDON AND NEW YORK

First published 2022
by Routledge
2 Park Square, Milton Park, Abingdon, Oxon OX14 4RN

and by Routledge
605 Third Avenue, New York, NY 10158

Routledge is an imprint of the Taylor & Francis Group, an informa business

© 2022 selection and editorial matter, Marian Gorynia, Barbara Jankowska and Katarzyna Mroczek-Dąbrowska; individual chapters, the contributors

The right of Marian Gorynia, Barbara Jankowska and Katarzyna Mroczek-Dąbrowska to be identified as the authors of the editorial material and of the authors for their individual chapters has been asserted in accordance with sections 77 and 78 of the Copyright, Designs and Patents Act 1988.

All rights reserved. No part of this book may be reprinted or reproduced or utilised in any form or by any electronic, mechanical, or other means, now known or hereafter invented, including photocopying and recording, or in any information storage or retrieval system, without permission in writing from the publishers.

Trademark notice: Product or corporate names may be trademarks or registered trademarks and are used only for identification and explanation without intent to infringe.

British Library Cataloguing-in-Publication Data
A catalogue record for this book is available from the British Library

Library of Congress Cataloging-in-Publication Data
Names: Gorynia, Marian, editor. | Jankowska, Barbara, editor. |
    Mroczek-Dąbrowska, Katarzyna, editor.
Title: Brexit and the future of the European Union : firm-level
    perspectives / edited by Marian Gorynia, Barbara Jankowska and
    Katarzyna Mroczek-Dąbrowska.
Description: Abingdon, Oxon ; New York, NY : Routledge, 2021. |
    Series: Routledge studies in the European economy | Includes
    bibliographical references and index.
Identifiers: LCCN 2021003946 (print) | LCCN 2021003947 (ebook)
Subjects: LCSH: European Union countries—Foreign economic
    relations—Great Britain. | European Union countries—Commerce—
    Great Britain. | European Union countries—Commercial policy. |
    European Union countries—Economic policy—21st century. |
    Industries—European Union countries. | Business enterprises—
    European Union countries.
Classification: LCC HC240.25.G7 B6925 2021 (print) | LCC
    HC240.25.G7 (ebook) | DDC 337.1/420941—dcundefined
LC record available at https://lccn.loc.gov/2021003946
LC ebook record available at https://lccn.loc.gov/2021003947

ISBN: 978-0-367-44261-3 (hbk)
ISBN: 978-1-032-04166-7 (pbk)
ISBN: 978-1-003-00860-6 (ebk)

Typeset in Bembo
by Apex CoVantage, LLC

Contents

Figures

Tables

Acknowledgments

This book would not be possible without the Publisher and the Series Editor who supported our idea from day one. We are grateful for all support on our quest to prepare the volume. We would like to thank all contributing authors who trusted us as we embarked on this, what turned out to be, a long and both professionally and privately adventurous journey. We would like to thank the entire Routledge team for the arduous technical assistance in the preparation of this volume for publication.

The monograph came into being within a research project financed by the National Science Centre, Poland No 2017/27/B/HS4/00754; title: Strategies of Polish companies against the UK's withdrawal from the European Union.

Editor biographies

Marian Gorynia, PhD, is Full Professor at the Poznań University of Economics and Business, Department of International Competitiveness. He was the Rector of the Poznań University of Economics and Business (2008–2016). His main research areas include international business [strategy of the firm in international business, international competitiveness of firms and industries and foreign direct investment (FDI)], strategic management and industrial organization. Professor Gorynia has published extensively in Polish and international scholarly journals and has authored or co-authored 20 books in his area of expertise. He has been serving on editorial boards of some journals: *Journal of Transnational Management Development, Journal of Transnational Management, Ekonomista*. He was a member of the Board of the European International Business Academy and a member of the Board of the International Management Development Association. He is the chairman of the Scientific Council of the Polish Economic Society.

Barbara Jankowska, PhD, is Full Professor at the Poznań University of Economics and Business, Poland, Head of the Department of International Competitiveness. She was the EIBA President for 2018. She is the National Representative of Poland in EIBA – European International Business Association, and the member of AIB – Academy of International Business, IT&FA – International Trade and Finance Association. Her research areas are international business (FDI, innovation performance of MNEs), Industry 4.0 and business clusters. Barbara Jankowska is an author and co-author of—research papers in (e.g.) *European Journal of International Management, European Planning Studies, Entrepreneurial Business and Economics Review, Journal of East European Management Studies, Post-Communist Economies* and of chapters published by (e.g.) Emerald, Routledge and Springer.

Katarzyna Mroczek-Dąbrowska, PhD, is Associate Professor at the Poznań University of Economics and Business, Department of International Competitiveness. Her main research areas include international competitiveness of firms and industries, transaction costs, and the internationalization process of industries. She is the author and co-author of published works covering amongst others the Global Financial Crisis and its impact on strategies of

Polish enterprises and the impact of Brexit on the EU-27 cohesion. Professor Mroczek-Dąbrowska is a member of the European International Business Academy and works on several international research and teaching projects cooperating with universities and consulting companies in the United Kingdom, Belgium, and Slovenia.

Contributors

Szymon Bytniewski is a Ph.D. candidate at the Poznań University of Economics and Business, Department of International Competitiveness. His main research areas include international business (strategy of the firm in international business, international competitiveness of firms, business models and business model adaptation during internationalization process).

John Cantwell is Distinguished Professor of International Business in Rutgers University (New Jersey, USA) since 2002. He was previously Professor of International Economics at the University of Reading in the UK. His early work helped to launch a new literature on multinational companies and international networks for technology creation, beyond merely international technology transfer. Professor Cantwell's total citation count on Google Scholar is currently around 20,000. His published research spans the fields of International Business and Management, Economics, Economic History, Economic Geography, Philosophy and Innovation Studies. Professor Cantwell served as the Editor-in-Chief of the *Journal of International Business Studies* (*JIBS*) from 2011 to 2016, which is the leading journal in the international business field. In 2019, he received the PWC Strategy & Eminent Scholar Award from the International Management Division of the Academy of Management for life-time achievement in international business scholarship. He was the elected Dean of the European International Business Academy (EIBA) Fellows from 2015 to 2018, and he is also an elected Fellow of the Academy of International Business (AIB) since 2005. In December 2021, he is due to receive an honorary doctorate (honoris causa) from Complutense University, Madrid, in recognition of his contributions to research.

Marlena Dzikowska, Ph.D., is Associate Professor at the Poznań University of Economics and Business, Department of International Competitiveness. Previously, she has been a visiting scholar at Copenhagen Business School, Denmark, the University of Glasgow, UK, and Zurich University of Applied Sciences, Switzerland. Her research interests include the role and evolution of subsidiaries, value chain management, relocation, and competitiveness. For her scientific work, she has won several international and national awards.

Cezary Główka, Ph.D., is Assistant Professor at the Poznań University of Economics and Business, Department of International Competitiveness. He is the coordinator of regional printing and advertising cluster organization, math teacher and entrepreneur. His main research areas include the influence of cluster organization on regional economies and vocational education. He was a founder member of Polish Cluster Association and Wielkopolska Clustering Centre. He worked for Polish Agency for Enterprise Development and Marshal Office of the Wielkopolska Region as an innovation broker and expert on clustering.

Aleksandra Kania, Ph.D., is Assistant Professor at the Poznań University of Economics and Business, Department of International Competitiveness. She is a former Rotary Scholar in Mannheim, Germany. For her doctoral thesis on innovative clusters in Baden-Württemberg and Greater Poland she won the first prize in the national competition funded by Wolters Kluwer.

Anna Matysek-Jędrych, Ph.D., is Assistant Professor at the Poznań University of Economics and Business, Department of International Competitiveness. Her main research areas include macroeconomics and political aspects of international economics. She is the Director of the Executive MBA Program held in cooperation with Georgia State University in Atlanta, United States. Dr Matysek-Jędrych's expertise covers financial markets, institutional framework and its impact on the economy's performance. Recently, she joined a research team on a project studying Brexit consequences on EU-27 cohesion and she conducts her own research in institutional determinants of macroprudential policy efficiency. She is the author of more than 50 scientific articles, chapters and monographs, including two research projects for the National Bank of Poland (winner of grant competition among economists from Poland). She is also a member of the editorial and review board of the *Journal of Eastern European and Central Asian Research* (Webster University), the *International Journal of Emerging Markets* and the *Cross-Cultural & Strategic Management*.

Ewa Mińska-Struzik, Ph.D., is Associate Professor in the Institute of International Business and Economics (Department of International Economics) at the Poznań University of Economics and Business in Poland. Since September 2019, she has been the Head of the Institute. Her main research area is international trade, which she studies from a macro perspective (with a particular focus on trade measurement, geographical concentration of trade flows and the validity of trade theories in a globalized world), as well on a micro level, exploring the linkage between exporting activity of a firm and its innovative potential. In her field of expertise, she is an author and co-author of journal articles (*Economics and Business Review, Gospodarka Narodowa. The Polish Journal of Economics, International Business and Global Economy, Wood. Research Papers. Reports. Announcements*), chapters, monographs, conference papers, textbooks, expert opinions and reports. In the years 2017–2018, she served as an expert for the European Commission (DG RTD) evaluating Fast Track to Innovation Programme under Horizon 2020. She is a member of the Board of Directors of The International Trade and Finance Association (2018–2020), the National Committee of the Economic Knowledge Contest (2017–2022) and the head of the Local Committee in Poznań.

Jan Polowczyk, Ph.D., is Associate Professor at Poznań University of Economics and Business, Department of International Competitiveness. His professional career has revolved around two major areas: academic and corporate. In 1993, he was invited to the corporate sphere and spent almost the next 18 years holding senior managerial positions in Polish affiliates of international companies and private business. In 2011, he returned to Academia. The main fields of his interests are: strategic management, international competitiveness, application of evolutionary and behavioral economics in management, merger and acquisitions. He is the author of more than 100 scientific articles, chapters and monographs. He has been serving on editorial boards of some journals: Scientific Journal Economics, Organisation and Management, and Visnik of Mariupol State University. He is a member of Strategic Management Society and Polish Economic Society. He worked on several international research and teaching projects with universities from the United Kingdom, Brasil, China, Ukraine and Bulgaria.

Piotr Trąpczyński, Ph.D., is Associate Professor at the Department of International Competitiveness, Poznań University of Economics and Business. His main research interests include the performance outcomes of firm internationalization and foreign market exits. He combines quantitative and qualitative methods in his research. He is author and co-author of academic papers published in leading international journals, such as *Journal of World Business, Journal of Business Research, International Business Review, European Management Journal* or *European Journal of International Management*. Professor Trąpczyński is co-founder and board member of the CEE Chapter of the Academy of International Business, and member of the Academy of International Business and European International Business Academy. Apart from academic research, he assisted numerous SMEs and MNEs in their international strategy development as Director of the International Business Center, which is part of the Knowledge Transfer Company of the Poznań University of Economics and Business.

Preface

Most of the analyses of Brexit have focused on the aggregate effects on international trade between Britain and the European Union (EU) depending upon various scenarios for the new terms on which trade takes place, and the consequent impacts on Gross Domestic Product, prices of traded goods and so on at a country level. This book is interesting since it extends this analysis from an aggregate or sectoral level to examine the implications for firm level strategies.

In this Preface to the book, I wish to consider two of the reasons why I think it makes an important contribution. The first is that the effects of Brexit on firms are likely to be very different depending on their context, and their strategic reactions to this major change in the trading environment are likely to differ too, and we need a better understanding of these variations across companies. The second is that the particular focus of this book on the relationship between Poland and Britain is highly relevant to an appreciation of the potential evolution of the Brexit effects over time in the future, in which the geographic composition of Britain's trade and investment with the EU countries may well undergo structural adjustment. I will argue that this may ultimately be to the advantage of at least some Polish firms by comparison with companies in other EU countries, which could eventually offset for them the detrimental initial effect of Brexit from which all parties are likely to suffer.

In support of each of these two reasons, I will refer to some previous work of my own. In the first case, some years ago, we examined the likely effects on FDI of increased European integration at the time of the development of the single market (Cantwell, 1992). We can suppose that these effects are symmetrical, so that a fall in the degree of cross-border integration due to Brexit simply has the reverse effects of a rise in integration. We contrasted the effects on market-seeking FDI, as opposed to internationally integrated FDI. If trade restrictions increase then market-seeking FDI may grow, as a means of jumping over the new trade barriers and continuing to serve a market currently reached through exporting. Instead, impediments to trade will adversely affect internationally integrated FDI, in which a subsidiary relies on substantial levels of both imports and exports between the home and host countries, as well as with third countries in the EU. This is just one of the explanations for why firm responses to Brexit will vary, and this book examines a range of other such influences.

With respect to the second reason for the significance of this book, Britain and Poland have long had a good relationship, going back at least to the Second World War. After the war, and again more recently, large numbers of Poles have settled in the UK. This is important because strong migration between two countries is another motivator of FDI. Pallavi Shukla and I have analyzed this effect in a recent article (Shukla & Cantwell, 2018). For brevity, I refer here especially to figure 1 on p. 839 in that paper, which illustrates our argument. Transient migration, associated with visiting families, or with periods of work or study abroad between Poland and Britain is likely to increase the institutional connectedness and hence relevant knowledge flows between these countries, which will help stimulate inward FDI into Britain from Poland. Having a sizeable established stock of migrants from Poland in Britain, as reflected, e.g., in the spread of Polish associations in Britain, creates greater institutional affinity between migrants' country of residence and their country of origin. This further enhances inward FDI in Britain by making it easier to develop better targeted applications with greater local market growth potential. We found that this role of increased institutional affinity is especially pertinent when the country of origin is at a lower level of economic development than the target country of residence, which applies to Poland and Britain.

What this suggests is that after Brexit, Poland may be at least in relative terms a winner compared to other EU countries, since Polish firms have a stronger foundation for expanding their position in the British market through FDI, despite Brexit. In our study, we controlled for the effects of trade agreements, so this influence of migration on FDI should hold independently of the direct impact of Brexit. Therefore, this makes the current volume especially appropriate to identifying the factors that are likely to differentiate the strategies of winners as opposed to losers in the aftermath of Brexit, which is one of the key issues raised by the authors of this book.

References

Cantwell, J. A. (1992). *Multinational investment in modern Europe: Strategic interaction in the integrated community*. Cheltenham: Edward Elgar.

Shukla, P., & Cantwell, J. A. (2018). Migrants and multinational firms: The role of institutional affinity and connectedness in FDI. *Journal of World Business*, *53*(6), 835–849. https://doi.org/10.1016/j.jwb.2018.07.003

1 Toward the new reality

EU after Brexit

Marian Gorynia, Barbara Jankowska,
Katarzyna Mroczek-Dąbrowska

Introduction

British voters' decision, made on June 23, 2016, to leave the European Union (EU) will visibly create a wide range of unpredictable consequences on the UK and other EU member states, the eurozone and the wider region. A vote for Brexit can be perceived as a starting point for the third round of the European crisis, following the eurozone debt crisis and the migration crisis. The result of the referendum generated, above all, quite a large shock to the British society and economy. Nevertheless, for the rest of the EU member states, Brexit would obviously not be a zero-sum game (cf. Miglbauer & Koller, 2019). Each of the EU countries will be hit by Brexit, to a smaller or larger extent though it is hard to predict the scale of the changes. Although Brexit is now a done deal, there is still much uncertainty over how it would impact the EU and national economies (Owen & Walter, 2017). Until the final agreement is signed, the unpredictability of the new rules is a cause for anxiety for companies involved in the British market.

In many EU countries, there should be a discernible impact on the companies' strategies caused by the British referendum. Since the UK withdrawal case is the first one in the EU's history, it creates uncertainty for all actors (small, large countries, EU institutions, societies, companies, etc.) and immediately after the referendum it was perceived as a significant rupture for the EU. Hence, the volume is driven by the strong belief that neither the UK nor the EU member states and institutions are interested in escalating tensions and the European disintegration process following Brexit (cf. King, 2020). All stakeholders in the Brexit negotiation process have had a stake in both the political and economic stability of Europe, which would ensure a safe environment for companies to continue their mutually beneficial cooperation (cf. Giammetti, 2020).

Key lines of argumentation advanced in this volume: questions and objectives

The problem discussed in the volume refers to the strategies that Polish companies implemented to cope with the volatility of external circumstances caused by the UK's withdrawal from the EU. The main objective is not to verify the changes caused by the Brexit itself but to study companies strategies in the post-vote and pre-Brexit period (2017–2019). Hence, the volume assesses whether companies have already developed strategies to face the new economic reality after Brexit or not and – if they have – how firms strived to tackle the uncertain future. Although Brexit is a fact now, we still cannot foresee its impact as the transition period is not over yet. Therefore, the volume's objectives include the following:

- to see how the trade-off between individual national goals and the European community so far impacted the negotiation process of Brexit;
- to see, in economic terms – which countries are bound (or not) to suffer most of the UK's withdrawal;
- to see how companies reacted to the imminent threat of Brexit and to distinguish the actual strategies they have adopted against Brexit; and
- to see which factors bore the most significant impact on their decisions regarding the British market.

The chapters included in this volume query current developments and processes that shape and influence the performance of companies' and their expansion paths today and in the future. The volume addresses the most topical issues that either delineate public discourse on Brexit and its consequences or should be included in that discourse but have been silenced, nevertheless. In this way, this volume "connects the dots" and uncovers the missing links necessary for any reader wishing to get a fuller understanding of the specificity of contemporary companies' strategies and EU integration. This volume addresses the under-researched area of company's response toward Brexit which so far has been mostly neglected.

The structure of the volume

The book consists of ten chapters, including this introductory chapter and the concluding one. The chapters address a variety of issues consistent with the volume's objectives. The discussion in the book takes a top-down approach, starting with the global perspective, to later on, focus on the company perspective. We discuss how the historical context influenced the genesis of Brexit and what implications this may have for the post-Brexit reality. We examine the economic ties that have existed between the UK and other member states, taking into consideration trade, investment and migration. These issues underpin the logic of the following chapters, which redirect the reader's attention to the company strategy. Based on the conclusions of Chapters 2 and 4, we assess which factors have so far impacted the company's strategies in the developed market (including the UK) and how the former studies go against the recent developments. In Chapters 7 and 8, we focus on the actual changes in the company's strategies in the British market and see which factors played the most important role in that process. In brief, this volume offers a rich and complex insight into today's state of art on companies' reply toward Brexit. The remainder of the book addresses the following issues.

To fully understand the genesis of Brexit, in Chapter 2, Anna Matysek-Jędrych and Katarzyna Mroczek-Dąbrowska outline the path and relations the UK has had with the EU. This chapter focuses on the tangled history and position the UK has taken throughout its years of EU membership. It outlines the main reasons for the referendum results covering the economic, political and social aspects of the Brexit. It also touches upon the multifaceted negotiation process which – even with Brexit being an accomplished fact – is still underway.

In Chapter 3, Marian Gorynia and Aleksandra Kania concentrate on the literature review regarding the potential economic outcome of the UK's withdrawal from the EU structures. The literature review revealed that most of the studies devoted to the Brexit's consequences focus on macroeconomic perspectives. These relate to the main freedoms gained by the EU accession: free movement of goods/services, persons and capital (Emerson, Busse, Di Salvo, Gros, & Pelkmans, 2017; Rojas-Romagosa, 2016). Much attention is devoted to the potential post-Brexit trade scenarios; in terms of both the UK's relations with the remaining EU-27 member states and the UK's relations with other countries. So far, an attempt has been made to assess the consequences of the UK's exit for the EU as a whole (Emerson et al., 2017) and for individual economies, e.g., the Netherlands (Rojas-Romagosa, 2016) or Ireland. However, with continued uncertainty over post-Brexit reality and with only a sketch of the future agreement, the question on mutual relations between the EU and the UK remains open.

Chapter 4, written by Katarzyna Mroczek-Dąbrowska and Anna Matysek-Jędrych, offers an analysis of the consequence of British voters' decision to withdraw from the EU through the lens of a disintegration process, by measuring the degree of vulnerability of the individual EU-27 countries (cf. Mroczek-Dąbrowska & Matysek-Jędrych, 2021). Although the UK's negotiations are held with the EU representing all 27 remaining member states, the impact it would have on individual economies can vary. The UK has a trade deficit (in goods) with the EU (around £70 billion), but not all countries are equally affected. If these surpluses were to be lost, large economies such as Germany, France, Italy or Spain are expected to suffer less than the small ones, like Luxemburg, Malta, the Netherlands, Belgium or Slovakia. This is due to the fact that – although in nominal values the exports of smaller countries to the UK is lower than the exports of the larger ones – their exports as a share of GDP is much higher. The common agreement seems to be the expectation that the long-term GDP of the UK (by 2030) will drop. The pessimistic scenarios forecast a reduction of more than 5% (Emerson et al., 2017; Begg, 2017). With the drop in UK's Gross Domestic Product (GDP), the Organization for Economic Cooperation and Development (OECD) also expects a drop of the EU-27 GDP, which by 2023 will fall by 0.8%. The chapter provides an economically rigorous and critical assessment of Brexit, with a focus on the ranking of potential winners and losers. Through the lens of the disintegration process, it contributes to the ongoing debate regarding the Brexit negotiation process by providing strong arguments in favor of or against certain solutions.

In Chapter 5, Barbara Jankowska and Anna Matysek-Jędrych and in Chapter 6 Marlena Dzikowska, Jan Polowczyk and Szymon Bytniewski write about an often overlooked but still essential dimension of the internationalization process: the strategies in the developed markets such as the British market. Companies internationalize with various reasons, entry modes and strategies. Their choices are often dictated by the market they approach; thus, their decisions (how) to enter developed markets will most certainly vary from the way they tackle the developing markets. To fully understand the implications Brexit can exert on the strategies of companies, it is first vital to have a look at the strategies the firms adopted in the times of relative stability. This chapters focus on the few main aspects: motives to internationalize, determinants of the internationalization process and specifics of internationalization process to the developed European countries. Based on the contribution made here, the empirical study on company's strategies toward Brexit could be developed.

Katarzyna Mroczek-Dąbrowska, Aleksandra Kania, Cezary Główka and Marian Gorynia, in Chapter 7, turn to the company perspective and offer an in-depth analysis of the post-vote but pre-Brexit strategies of companies in the British market. The research focuses mostly on the impact the exogenous factors (policy changes, taxation, trade barriers, etc.) may have had on the strategy making. This chapter presents the results of the empirical research based on primary study and conducted on a sample of Polish companies. The factors under study include market, cost, competitive and governmental determinants. This chapter links directly to Chapter 5, where such dependencies are discussed in conceptual manner.

In Chapter 8, Barbara Jankowska, Katarzyna Mroczek-Dąbrowska and Aleksandra Kania offer a typology of the strategies adopted by companies in the face of Brexit. The study is based on the same sample that served for discussion in Chapter 7. In reference to Ansoff's matrix, the authors verify how companies behaved already having the knowledge of Brexit but still uncertain of the exact shape of the "divorce". The results hint to certain patterns (industries, company size, entry mode, etc.) that distinguished particular strategies.

Chapter 9, written by Barbara Jankowska, Aleksandra Kania and Piotr Trąpczyński, supplements the studies on company behavior with quantitative perspective. Qualitative research allows us to examine the Brexit phenomenon in its proper context, by providing a more detailed description and exemplifying the relationships described as part of quantitative research. At the same time, collecting qualitative data enables us to triangulate the conclusions formulated in the earlier stages of the research process. Furthermore, case study analysis allows us to verify to what extent the generalized conclusions on Brexit and observations in the quantitative results are confirmed by selected real-life business cases. The data were acquired by means of an interview questionnaire with questions concerning all the sections studied in Chapters 7 and 9, and they are supplemented with direct interviews aimed at extending some of the topics from the questionnaire.

In Chapter 10, Marian Gorynia, Barbara Jankowska and Katarzyna Mroczek-Dąbrowska draw the conclusions that wrap up the discussion on company's position toward Brexit. Companies constitute the core of the economic relations between the UK and the EU, and the changes that happen within them have a direct impact on the society by shaping the labor market, migration trends, consumption and others. Companies cannot be neglected as their response to new reality may backfire – either to the EU, the UK or possibly to both.

Conclusions

The microeconomic perspective on Brexit – focusing on its impact on the companies' strategies – is of utmost importance for the EU members which overall have very close economic relations with the UK. Most companies perceive Brexit as an inconvenience if not a threat which therefore requires adaptive moves. At the same time, companies do not suffer from and respond to the change in the same way. There is hardly any research on company strategies in the face of Brexit. One of the reasons for that is limited data availability. Information on approaches toward Brexit cannot be found in any official statistical data and requires in-depth analysis at the core of the setting – the company. However, this requires time and other resources. This volume aims to understand the different approaches toward the UK's exit and understand its meaning for the whole economy. The study encompasses a complex and multidimensional research workshop based on a distinct yet simultaneously co-related areas, such as the theory of the firm, international business, along with micro- and macroeconomics.

References

Begg, I. (2017). Making sense of the costs and benefits of Brexit: Challenges for economists. *Atlantic Economic Journal*, *45*, 299–315. https://doi.org/10.1007/s11293-017-9550-x

Emerson, M., Busse, M., Di Salvo, M., Gros, D., & Pelkmans, J. (2017). *An assessment of the economic impact of Brexit on the EU27*. Brussels: Centre for European Policy Studies (CEPS), IP/A/IMCO/2016-2013.

Giammetti, R. (2020). Tariffs, domestic import substitution and trade diversion in input-output production networks: An exercise on Brexit. *Economic Systems Research*, *32*(3), 318–350. https://doi.org/10.1080/09535314.2020.1738347

King, R. (2020). On Europe, immigration and inequality: Brexit as a "wicked problem". *Journal of Immigrant & Refugee Studies*, *19*(1), 25–38. https://doi.org/10.1080/15562948.2020.1821275

Miglbauer, M., & Koller, V. (2019). 'The British people have spoken': Voter motivations and identities in vox pops on the British EU referendum. In V. Koller, S. Kopf, & M. Miglbauer (Eds.), *Discourses of Brexit*. Oxon & New York: Routledge.

Mroczek-Dąbrowska, K., & Matysek-Jędrych, A. (2021). "To fear or not to fear?" The nature of the EU-27 countries' vulnerability to Brexit. *European Planning Studies*, *29*(2), 277–290. https://doi.org/10.1080/09654313.2020.1745761

Owen, E., & Walter, S. (2017). Open economy politics and Brexit: Insights, puzzles, and ways forward. *Review of International Political Economy*, *24*(2), 179–202. https://doi.org/10.1080/09692290.2017.1307245

Rojas-Romagosa, H. (2016). *Trade effects of Brexit for the Netherlands. Copenhagen.* CPB Netherlands Bureau for Economic Policy Analysis. Retrieved from www.cpb.nl/sites/default/files/omnidownload/CPB-Backgroud-Document-June-2016-Trade-effects-of-brexit-for-the-netherlands.pdf

2 The UK versus Brexit

Introduction to comprehensive analysis

Anna Matysek-Jędrych,
Katarzyna Mroczek-Dąbrowska

The economic, political and social place of the UK in the EU

The UK became a member of the European Community only on January 1, 1973. However, the UK's links with continental Europe and its desire for integration date many years back. The British recognized the importance of cooperation in Europe already directly after the Second World War. It took time to establish the scope and form of this cooperation. The first step toward the integration of the UK with other countries was the co-founding of the European Movement International in 1948: a non-governmental association that lobbied for the strengthening of political, social and economic ties in Europe. Despite the undoubted recognition of European integration, the UK did not join the European Coal and Steel Community (ECSC), established in 1952. This restraint stemmed from British fears for the loss of "national identity," the low volume of trade with European countries in comparison with non-European states, and close ties with the United States (Rozenek, 2012, p. 101). Concerns about the enlargement of the European Community also arose in continental Europe. Europeans believed that close relations between the UK and the Americans could lead to their excessive interference in the course of affairs in the Old World. However, after the establishment of the European Economic Community (EEC) in 1957, the UK began to seek alternative alliances that would counterbalance US influence in Europe. Together with Austria, Denmark, Norway, Sweden, Switzerland and Portugal, the UK has created a so-called small trade zone known as EFTA, which stands for the European Free Trade Association. Hence, despite tightening trade links with these countries and despite the Euroskepticism of its citizens, the UK began efforts to join the European Community. These efforts finally succeeded in 1973. However, in retrospect, it is estimated that the main reason for the UK's accession to the EU was to balance influence and prevent the emergence of a dominant power, or a group of powers, in Europe. We may characterize that reason as a political factor, which makes Britain's motivation differ from that of many other members.

Despite the undoubtedly high political and economic importance of the UK in Europe and the world, its accession to the European Community was turbulent and relatively long. Therefore, it is unsurprising that the final conditions of accession were significantly different from those negotiated by other member states. The UK had the opportunity to use the so-called *opt-out* in several important EU policies. It was the case with the Schengen Agreement, the Economic and Monetary Union, the Charter of Fundamental Rights, and the sphere of freedom, security, and justice.

As mentioned earlier, the specific role of the UK in the EU resulted from historical circumstances, established political and economic priorities, and the distinct individualism of the British (Rozenek, 2012). Although social, political and economic spheres of life are significantly interlinked, only some of them dominated the UK's attitude and actions at different times.

Political and social aspects of the UK's functioning in the EU

Social moods significantly determine the political scene of a given country and, for many years, the UK has been no exception. Social attitude toward integration with the rest of Europe has fueled the governing parties' activities, in both internal politics and relations with the EU. Although 45 years have passed since the UK joined the EU and individual governments have taken slightly different positions on the strengthening of European ties, we notice some shared elements of this period, which dominated the image and role of the UK in the European Community.

To properly understand the UK's position toward the EU, we should remember what exactly the UK is. It consists of four countries: England, Scotland, Wales and Northern Ireland. Moreover, it also has non-UK-dependent territories and overseas territories, none of which were part of the EU. The UK was a post-colonial empire, and it still maintains close relations with many overseas territories, despite its loss of power. Along with geographical isolation from continental Europe, post-colonial history has reinforced the sense of British individualism over the years. The UK was the third most populated country in the EU, with about 13% of the EU population. The process of immigration to the UK, initiated by the 1950s crisis, has resulted in the diversification of its inhabitants in terms of culture, ethnicity and worldviews.

Despite social diversity, the British for many years proved Euroskeptic, if not indifferent to integration. One of the manifestations of this attitude is the lateness of Britain's accession to the European Community. However, this fact had major consequences for the political role that the UK played in European circles. Many of the EU institutions were already well-established, and the UK could not play such a role in their formation as it could expect as a major European player. Thus, many perceived the UK as an outsider who only involved in those policies that were crucial to the UK itself. These include, above all, the single market, the issue of the EU enlargement to include Central and Eastern European countries, the Common Commercial Policy, and to some extent, the Common Foreign and Security Policy (Rozenek, 2012, p. 116).

The issue of the UK adopting the euro, the common currency of the EU, has been one of the bones of contention between Brussels and London. The UK has negotiated an opt-out option, which means that it has retained the possibility to choose whether to join the euro area after it would meet the euro convergence criteria. The UK's reluctance to adopt the single currency was primarily due to the fear of the loss of shock-absorbing tools and autonomy in monetary policy (Mrzygłód, 2010, pp. 161–162). Skeptics highlighted such issues as the incompatibility of business cycles and the economic structure of the euro area countries and that of the UK, along with the insufficient flexibility of the economy, including the labor market. The former part of the argument lost its relevance after 2004, as these economies started developing at a similar pace thanks to the process of globalization. However, at the same time, experts acknowledged that the adoption of the euro would result in increased inflows of FDI, along with an increase in trade. Experts also believed that the UK's financial market would strengthen, the importance of the City of London would increase, and there would occur long-term positive impact on production and employment (Mrzygłód, 2010, p. 160). However, referendum results determined the adoption of the single currency, and survey results showed that the British would not agree to abandon the pound. In 2009, 75% of those surveyed declared that they would vote against the adoption of the euro.

British Euroskepticism was a commonly known fact. As early as in 1975, two years after the UK joined the European Community, there was a referendum to decide whether to remain in the organization. The result of 67% of votes in support of remaining in the EU was decisive for the strengthening of relations for the next decades. However, negative or at best ambivalent attitudes toward the EU organized domestic politics, and Euroskepticism manifested itself in the position of individual governments. In 2016, 51.9% of the voters who took part in the referendum decided that the UK should not stay in the EU, which determined the separation of the country from the organization. However, it is worth mentioning that results varied from country to country: in Scotland and Northern Ireland, pro-EU attitudes prevailed, while Wales and England voted to leave EU structures (see Table 2.1). It means that although the Europeans generally perceive the British as Euroskeptics, the British are nevertheless internally diverse as a community of countries.

Economic aspects of the UK's functioning in the EU

The UK is undoubtedly one of the most important economies, in both Europe and the world. Its Anglo-Saxon model bases on a liberal concept, according to which the interference of institutions and the state in the economy's functioning is limited to a minimum (Woś, 2001, p. 175). The UK was one of the largest contributors to the EU budget, alongside France and Germany. Between 2000 and 2016, the UK contributed a total of almost EUR 180.8 billion to the common budget (European Commission, 2018). In the calculation of the UK's due contributions, we should mention that in 1984, under Margaret Thatcher, the

Table 2.1 Comparison of the results of referenda on the UK staying in the EU (2016 versus 1975)

Location	Votes for "leave"	Votes for "remain"	Turnout
2016			
England	53.4%	46.6%	73%
Northern Ireland	44.2%	55.8%	62.7%
Scotland	38%	62%	67.2%
Wales	52.5%	47.5%	71.7%
1975			
England	31.4%	68.6%	64.6%
Northern Ireland	47.8%	52.2%	47.4%
Scotland	42.6%	58.4%	61.7%
Wales	35.2%	64.8%	66.9%

Source: Own elaboration based on Miller (2015) and Electoral Commission (2016).

UK was granted a so-called UK rebate, i.e., an annual reduction in its membership contribution to the budget. The reasons why the EU granted the UK rebate were as follows (Rozenek, 2012, pp. 110–111):

• the UK's small agricultural sector, and hence the EU's low level of expenditure on the country's agriculture and
• the relatively high level of financing of the European Community budget from the high share of national GNP in the VAT tax base.

The UK rebate was covered by other member states, especially Germany, France, the Netherlands and Sweden bore a significant burden of the compensation. Figure 2.1 illustrates the contributions of the UK, Germany and France to the EU budget in 2000–2016.

What is important is not only the analysis of membership fees but also information on how much of the EU budget the UK did receive. Throughout the analyzed period, except for the year 2001, the UK was a net contributor, which means that its contribution to the European budget exceeded its expenditure (Table 2.2). In the period from 2000 to 2006, the British allocated an average of 58% of subsidies to support agriculture, 30% to structural measures, 10% to internal policies, and the remaining amount to administration. From 2007 to 2013, after changes in expenditure categories, the British allocated about 58% of the funds to natural resources management and 38% to the development of competitiveness and cohesion. The UK allocated the rest to the administration and the spheres of citizenship, freedom, security and justice. As part of its latest allocations, in 2014–2016, the UK spent on average 54% of subsidies on the sustainable development of natural resources and 42% on smart economic

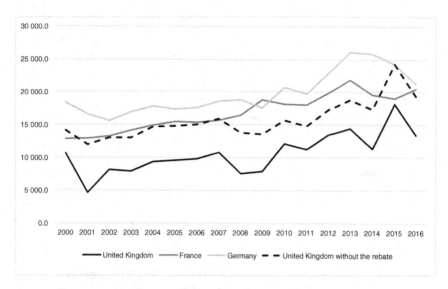

Figure 2.1 Payments to the EU budget in 2000–2016 in EUR millions

Table 2.2 The UK's revenues and expenses in 2000–2016 (in EUR billions)

	2000	2001	2002	2003	2004	2005	2006	2007	2008	2009	2010	2011	2012	2013	2014	2015	2016
R	10.7	4.6	8.1	7.9	9.4	9.6	9.8	10.8	7.6	7.9	12.1	11.3	13.5	14.5	11.3	18.2	13.5
E	7.9	5.9	6.2	6.2	7.1	8.7	8.3	7.4	7.3	6.2	6.7	6.6	6.9	6.3	7.0	7.5	7.1
Net	2.8	−1.2	1.9	1.7	2.2	1.0	1.5	3.3	0.3	1.6	5.4	4.7	6.5	8.2	4.4	10.8	6.4

Source: European Commission (2018).
E: the UK's expenditure from the EU budget; R: the UK's payments to the EU.

growth supporting social inclusion. The UK spent the rest on security, citizenship and administration.

Directly not the largest beneficiary of EU funds, the UK economy sought other possibilities to cooperate with the rest of the European Community. One of the most prominent methods was foreign trade. The EU remains the UK's most important trading partner, but the EU's share of British companies' exports fell from 55% in 2006 to 43% in 2016. Since the referendum in 2016, experts have observed a reversal of the pro-integration trend, and the share of non-EU countries in British exports exceeded 55% in 2017. Experts have drawn similar conclusions based on the analysis of import trends, in which the share of EU countries in British imports fell from 58% in 2002 to 54% in 2016. Therefore, the UK has a trade deficit with members of the EU. The UK mainly exports services, especially financial services in the broadest sense, whereas it imports goods. We will discuss detailed figures for the UK's foreign trade with individual EU members in greater detail in Chapter 4, so we will present below only the most important facts.

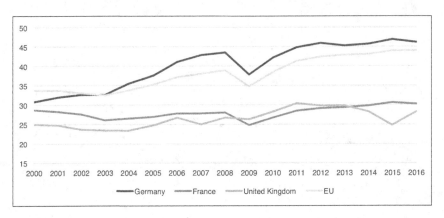

Figure 2.2 Value of exports of selected EU countries in 2000–2016 (in % of GDP)

Source: OECD (2018).

However, if one analyses exports in relation to the GDP generated by the country, it turns out that, in 2000–2016, the UK was the least dependent on exports out of all EU members. The UK exports in the analyzed period amounted to only 26.4% of GDP, while the average for the whole EU was 38.1% (Figure 2.2). Obviously, small countries such as Luxembourg, Ireland or Slovakia were highly dependent on foreign trade because demand in their home markets was insufficient. In contrast, large countries such as France, Italy and the UK generally displayed the opposite dependence.

Another pillar on which the cooperation between the UK and the EU relied was FDI. Thanks to a stable institutional environment and favorable regulations for investors, the UK was an important location for investments. At the same time, British entrepreneurs were eager to invest abroad (Table 2.3). The value of British investment abroad amounted to £1.2 trillion in 2016, and the increase in this value occurred mainly thanks to mergers and acquisitions in recent years. The investment value in the UK also reached almost £1.2 trillion.

The UK has significant capital ties to Europe, especially to the EU. The EU remains the number one investment direction for the British, but also as a recipient of investments from other member states. Interestingly, the Netherlands, Luxembourg and France remain the UK's main partners in both inbound and outbound investments. However, from the perspective of the period of 2007–2016, we see that British companies have started to look for non-European investment directions, and they concentrated their focus especially on Asia.

We could also show the UK-EU links in other economic fields. However, the aim of this subchapter is not to analyze all possible aspects of these relations but to show that despite the British Euroskeptic attitude, the UK is one of the most important elements of the European economy (Corbett, 2016). Thus, the results of the Brexit referendum will have serious consequences both for the leaving country and for the other members of the EU.

Table 2.3 The UK's outward investment position and inward investment position – the geographical breakdown

Year	Europe	UE	North and South Americas	Asia	Australia and Oceania	Africa
Outward investment position						
2007	59.37%	46.55%	30.98%	5.53%	1.88%	2.24%
2008	59.87%	48.07%	30.15%	6.43%	1.78%	1.77%
2009	57.78%	49.70%	29.19%	7.52%	1.89%	3.61%
2010	59.90%	52.42%	24.48%	9.34%	3.16%	3.12%
2011	57.56%	49.86%	25.77%	9.98%	3.55%	3.13%
2012	54.60%	47.03%	27.36%	10.04%	4.05%	3.95%
2013	50.60%	41.71%	29.96%	11.46%	4.64%	3.34%
2014	48.69%	41.26%	34.07%	11.25%	2.02%	3.96%
2015	49.27%	42.08%	31.63%	12.75%	2.76%	3.59%
2016	51.07%	43.38%	29.18%	12.56%	3.47%	3.72%
Inward investment position						
2007	58.33%	51.80%	31.53%	8.37%	1.53%	0.24%
2008	58.22%	50.78%	33.54%	6.79%	1.12%	0.32%
2009	61.19%	54.34%	31.16%	5.67%	1.81%	0.16%
2010	58.45%	50.92%	33.29%	6.82%	1.23%	0.21%
2011	57.61%	48.94%	33.12%	7.58%	1.45%	0.24%
2012	59.25%	49.54%	32.83%	6.87%	0.90%	0.15%
2013	60.75%	50.34%	30.44%	8.12%	0.43%	0.26%
2014	59.31%	48.38%	31.94%	7.30%	1.17%	0.28%
2015	52.72%	42.69%	37.63%	7.95%	1.46%	0.24%
2016	56.33%	45.15%	34.36%	8.06%	1.09%	0.16%

Source: own elaboration based on Office for National Statistics (2020).

The meaning of the term "Brexit" and the origins of the process

The term "Brexit" is commonly used from June 23, 2016, which is the date of the referendum on the UK's withdrawal from the EU. We will use the term Brexit in this monograph, for which it is key. Therefore, we wish to provide an in-depth analysis of the semantic differences that form the basis for the full understanding of the term Brexit in legal, political, economic and social perspectives. Brexit is the result of decomposition in word formation which, on the one hand, is supposed to fill an identified semantic gap and, on the other hand, it is supposed to attract attention. In the case of "Brexit," two English words have been put together: "Britain" and "exit". Interestingly, according to Oxford Dictionaries, the word appeared already in 2012, initially as "Brixit". Its prototype was the word "Grexit". After all, Greece was the first country to consider leaving the EU as a result of growing economic problems, which culminated in a deep debt crisis (for more, see Featherstone, 2011; Lane, 2012; De Santis, 2012).

Hence, how to understand the term Brexit? We can do as Theresa May proposed in her speech just 20 days after the referendum: "Brexit means Brexit" (Cowburn, 2016). In the colloquial and narrow sense, "Brexit" is used to describe the decision taken in the referendum and the referendum itself. But it is not the correct understanding. "Brexit" is not a one-time event but a long-term process, and this is how we should perceive the term. Noteworthy, the term "Brexit" functioned in the mass media long before the mentioned referendum. It left almost no room for another word, "Bremain," which is a combination of two other British words: "Britain" and "remain". The word suggested that the UK should stay in the EU. At this point, we should ask what impact each term had on the referendum's outcome when we consider the peculiar asymmetry in the use of both terms in the period directly preceding the event. However, as interesting as it may be, this matter far exceeds the scope of this study.

In a broader sense, Brexit determines the whole process of the UK's withdrawal from the EU, if we consider the multidimensionality of the potential consequences of this process (Szymczyński, 2016). Therefore, the process affects not only the UK as a country whose citizens made a democratic decision to leave the EU but also all other EU member states in macroeconomic, microeconomic, political, social, legal and other dimensions. In the macroeconomic dimension, Brexit should refer to the consequences of the UK's withdrawal from the EU concerning the economic position of this country, measured by, e.g., GDP growth, foreign trade dynamics, the value of the British currency. Moreover, Brexit should refer to the economic position of the EU without the UK as a member state. The microeconomic aspect covers individual companies, households and individual workers of those institutions that operate in the UK and are somehow affected by the decision to leave the EU. This aspect also covers all those who will be indirectly affected by the decision from June 2016.

Let us consider the legal aspect of the Brexit process, understood as forced changes in the legal system of both the UK and the EU, along with the determination of interdependencies between the two legal systems. It is probably the most complicated among all the aspects of Brexit, and the number and scale of importance of related issues fully reflect the degree of complexity as follows (Gordon & Moffatt, 2016; Miller, 2016):

- To what amplitude will we witness the repeal or amendment of legislation presently in force that gives effect to the EU regulations?
- How big fraction of the EU law will be transposed into domestic law after the UK leaves the EU?
- Wherever EU legislation is transposed into domestic law, will the law be kept in concordance with any changes made by the EU?

- What will be the proportion to which changes to legislation to give effect to Brexit will be set out in primary legislation?
- Will the "Great Repeal Bill" simply transpose EU law into domestic law after Brexit?
- Will the UK courts continue to enforce the jurisprudence of the Court of Justice of the EU when interpreting EU law after it has been transposed into domestic law?

The social dimension of the Brexit process can be considered on two levels: ex post and ex ante. The former includes in-depth studies on the social and cultural characteristics of a group of British people who voted for the UK's exit from the EU (see Goodwin & Heath, 2016; Startin, 2015). The latter is much more important because it exceeds the assessment of the current state: it covers the social consequences yet to be reflected in tendencies that shape tensions among social groups in relation to age, gender, the standard of living or education (see Henderson et al., 2016; Kenny, 2016; Leconte, 2015), not to mention the nationalist and populist movements that will arise in Europe after Brexit.

To understand the very concept of Brexit is the first step to an in-depth analysis of this process; no less important is to explain the origin of the process itself. A retrospective look at the process of European integration allows us to see the distinctive features of the UK and mainland Europe. The British particularly highlighted this distinction as seen, e.g., in the words of Ernest Bevin, the British Foreign Secretary in the postwar period: "We must remain, as we have always been in the past, different in character from other European nations and fundamentally incapable of wholehearted integration with them" (Berend, 2016, p. 41). The main threats that the British saw in the integration of Europe were as follows (Blackwell, 1993; Radwan, 2015; Wilkes, 1997): the independence of the British Parliament, the future of the Commonwealth, the position of the working class in the future united Europe and integration based on ideas from Germany and France with the exception of the UK. The almost inborn aversion to supranational power was not irrelevant to the assessment of European integration by the British, even more when this power resulted not from democratic elections.

The UK's participation in the successive stages of integration, including the ECSC, the EEC, the EU, and the eurozone, only confirms the high level of Euroskepticism among the British. Initially, the UK did not join the ECSC and the EEC but then had to face the veto of Charles De Gaulle when the country applied for admission to the EEC in 1961. It was only in 1973 that the UK, together with Denmark and Ireland, became member states of the European Communities. The UK did not participate in the subsequent stages of integration, which included the signing of the Schengen Agreement and the creation of the euro area with the single currency – the euro – and the creation of the European Central Bank. Already at these stages, the British people clearly emphasized their autonomy, or even separateness, from the countries of mainland Europe.

Pro-European sentiment in the UK has fluctuated, but even under Prime Minister Tony Blair, whom Europeans perceived as an avowed European, interested parties did not strengthen the monetary integration of the UK into continental Europe. The issue of the common currency never raised the British interest (cf. Kenny, 2016; Mikołajczyk, 2016). It seems that Brexit is an integral part of the UK's integration process into Europe and, at the same time, that the scenario of the country's withdrawal from European structures was predictable. The words of the mid-nineteenth-century UK Prime Minister, Henry Palmerston, perfectly illustrate the attitude of the British toward other nations: "We have no eternal allies, and we have no perpetual enemies. Our interests are eternal and perpetual, and those interests it is our duty to follow" (Frost, 2018, p. 196).

The course of the Brexit process

The referendum held on June 23, 2016, and especially its result was only the first step in the long-term process of the UK's withdrawal from the EU. Article 50 of the Treaty on EU requires a state that decides to leave the EU structures to formally inform the European Council of its intention. This formal act means the actual beginning of the process of negotiating the conditions for leaving the EU. The European Commission conducts the negotiations on behalf of the EU and approves the agreement's final form with a vote. These negotiations are between representatives of the UK and the European Commission. The process requires the European Commission to present a progress report to both the European Council and the European Parliament. Once the UK has agreed on the conditions for leaving the EU, the agreement requires the approval of the European Parliament, while the negotiation's conclusion happens with the agreement of all 27 member states that remain in the EU (Mance, Baker, & Parker, 2018). Due to negotiation difficulties, both sides have postponed the dates for the subsequent stages of the UK's withdrawal from the European Community multiple times. Although Brexit finally became a reality on January 31, 2020, the UK's divorce from the EU is still not complete. Despite the signing of the so-called Withdrawal Agreement, interested parties did not establish the final shape of the Brussels-London relationship (Table 2.4).

The situation regarding the Brexit process is extremely dynamic and depends on the decisions of individual bodies at different levels of the EU and the UK. Hence, the schedule presented in Table 2.3 has been subject to numerous changes. Interested parties have many times postponed the date of the UK's withdrawal from the EU, which led to increased uncertainty across Europe. Eventually, the UK left the EU structures on January 31, 2020. Still, the uncertainty that this fact has caused has not diminished, because the future principles on which the relationship between the UK and the EU should base remain unknown.

Table 2.4 Assumed course of the Brexit process (as of July 2020)

Deadline	UK	EU
June 23, 2016	The UK holds a referendum on its membership of the EU	
July 13, 2016	Theresa May becomes the new UK Prime Minister	
February 2, 2017	The government publishes its Brexit White Paper, formally setting out its strategy for exiting the EU	
March 29, 2017	Theresa May notifies the European Council President Donald Tusk of the UK's intention to leave the EU	
March 31, 2017		The President of the European Council publishes draft negotiation guidelines for the "EU-27" (the EU members excluding the UK)
June 19, 2017	First round of UK-EU exit negotiations	
December 8, 2017	UK and EU publish a Joint Report on progress made during Phase 1 of negotiations	
January–June 2018	The EU (Withdrawal) Bill is processed in the House of Lords and Parliament	
August 23, 2018	The government publishes the first collection of technical notices providing guidance on how to prepare for a no-deal Brexit	
November 25, 2018		At a special meeting of the European Council, EU-27 leaders endorse the Withdrawal Agreement and approve the political declaration on future EU-UK relations
January–March 2019	The Prime Minister presents *Plan B* on Brexit deal, suffers defeat in House of Commons and seeks permission from the EU to extend Article 50	
March 21, 2019		Following a meeting of the European Council, EU-27 leaders agree to grant an extension comprising two possible dates: May 22, 2019, should the Withdrawal Agreement gain approval from MPs next week; or April 12, 2019, should the Withdrawal Agreement not be approved by the House of Commons

(Continued)

Table 2.4 (Continued)

Deadline	UK	EU
April 10, 2019		European Council meeting. Theresa May asks for an extension of Article 50 until the end of June. The Council then meets in an EU27 format to discuss the Prime Minister's proposal. The UK and EU27 later agree a further extension of Article 50 until October 31, 2019, but with the possibility of leaving earlier if the Withdrawal Agreement is ratified by both parties before this date
July 24, 2019	Boris Johnson formally takes over as Prime Minister	
September–December 2019	Proceeding of the EU (Withdrawal Agreement) Bill in various legislative bodies in the UK	
January 31, 2020	At 11:00 p.m., the UK leaves the EU and enters the transition period	
February 1, 2020	The transition period begins	
March 2–5, 2020	First round up UK-EU future relationship negotiations	
April 20–24, 2020	Second round up UK-EU future relationship negotiations	
May 11–15, 2020	Third round up UK-EU future relationship negotiations	
June 2–5, 2020	Fourth round up UK-EU future relationship negotiations	
June 30, 2020	Deadline for the UK to request an extension of the transition period beyond 2020	
July–October 2020	Further UK-EU negotiating rounds	
December 31, 2020	Date in law for the transition period to end	
January 1, 2021	New agreement on UK-EU relations should enter into force (if an agreement has been reached and ratified by the end of 2020)	

Source: Own elaboration based on Walker (2020).

Possible scenarios of the future relations between the UK and the EU

As part of the negotiation process between the UK and the EU, the most important element will be to reformulate relations between the EU and the UK. The literature lists at least seven different scenarios, some of which are copies of solutions that the EU currently uses for other countries, such as Norway, Switzerland and Turkey. The other scenarios are hybrids of existing solutions (Howarth & Quaglia, 2017; Piris, 2016). The negotiations considered various scenarios:

* a non-standard solution adjusted to the needs of the UK and the EU, i.e., relations developed from scratch;

- the UK's membership in the European Free Trade Agreement (EFTA), which the UK left in 1973 as a result of its accession to the EU;
- the UK's membership in the European Economic Area (EEA), which is the so-called "Norwegian model";
- the so-called "Swiss model" based on bilateral trade agreements between the UK and the EU;
- the so-called "Turkish model" based on the customs union with the EU;
- a free trade agreement with the EU; and
- a relationship between the two partners based on World Trade Organization (WTO) rules.

The first scenario is extremely difficult to negotiate. The UK will seek to recognize elements beneficial to the British economy but, at the same time, exclude those that the British society opposes. In turn, the EU representatives process may only try to promote solutions that will satisfy the EU institutions and individual member states. Therefore, it may turn out that there will be no possibility to develop new relations without significant concessions from both sides.

The second scenario assumes that the UK would only be a member of the EFTA: the UK already was a member of the EFTA until 1973. The EFTA membership would give the UK extremely narrowly defined economic benefits, including those that result from a free trade agreement on selected agricultural products and fish. The EFTA has basically stopped its development as a supranational institutional solution as it was replaced by the EEA, which is a much more far-reaching solution in terms of economic integration and cooperation. Therefore, we should consider the UK's membership in the EFTA as a mere theoretical solution, which is not very much justified in the practice of future UK-EU relations development due to the limited scale of economic benefits.

The third scenario assumes the UK's membership in the EEA and the formation of relations between the UK and the EU based on solutions already applied in the case of Norway. Membership in the EEA would provide the UK with access to the European single market and the possibility to implement rules on the free movement of goods,[1] services, capital and the labor factor. The UK would be able to apply these rules without the need to participate in a common European policy on, among other things, agriculture, fisheries, justice, foreign policy and other common EU policies. At the same time, access to the single market requires compliance with existing and future regulations. The UK will only be able to express an opinion on them without a direct influence on the adopted institutional and legal arrangements.[2] The UK will also have to agree to a significant tightening of trade policy.

Another applicable option was to adopt for the UK the perspective of solutions implemented in practice by Switzerland, which is the so-called "Swiss model". In this case, cooperation with the EU would rely on more than 120 sectoral agreements, several of which are of crucial importance, while instead narrowly define the principles of cooperation. However, from the UK perspective it seems most important that cooperation concerning the broader service sector is still largely unregulated, which especially applies to financial services, except for life insurance services. Financial services are particularly important to the UK because of London's leading role as an international financial center. Furthermore, the adoption of the "Swiss model" would entail a high level of uncertainty as to how the interested parties will shape future relations. We should expect changes in relations between Switzerland and the EU,[3] as is the case with the EEA.

The "Turkish model" as the basis for shaping relations between the UK and the EU would consider the functioning of the countries within a customs union. Therefore, interested parties would abolish internal customs tariffs. However, they would still be obligated to apply the same external tariffs developed under the agreement to relations with third countries. From the viewpoint of the UK, the customs union would imply the need to accept external customs tariffs imposed by the EU without full access to the Common Market due to the exclusion of the services sector from that union. We should address another serious criticism against the customs union and the functioning of the UK within such a union, which concerns FTAs negotiated by the EU. The UK would be unable to approve the FTAs or benefit from them fully.[4]

Another institutional option for future relations between the UK and the EU involves the signature of a free trade agreement. If we analyze the future institutional arrangements between the EU and the UK economies and their mutual importance, this appears like a very likely scenario for the future. We should emphasize that all the agreements signed so far by the EU do not address the matter with enough complexity to serve as a starting point for the negotiation process. Both the agreement negotiated with Singapore and the one negotiated with Canada do not include characteristics that arise from the functioning of the European single market. The UK's admission to the Common Market would undoubtedly require the acceptance and adaptation of future EU regulations related to the internal market in its broadest sense. Among other things, these regulations include competition law regulations, consumer health and safety protection, technical specifications of products and the standards these products must meet.

The last possible scenario assumed that the cooperation between the UK and the EU would be based solely on WTO rules. Two issues seem crucial in the process of considering this option as a possible future. First, the WTO has so far been ineffective in the elimination of tariff and non-tariff barriers (NTBs) to foreign trade. Second, the UK's withdrawal from the EU means that the former automatically renounces its participation in more than 60 FTAs negotiated so far by the EU. These FTAs represent about 35% of world trade. The second issue will be a topic of concern in each of the aforementioned scenarios.

Table 2.5 summarizes the aforementioned scenarios, together with their impact on future relations between the UK and the EU. The differences between the solutions are significant and, in some cases, extreme. We can

Table 2.5 Implications of various options for the future EU-UK relationship

Options	No Brexit	EFTA	EEA (Norway)	Swiss model	CU (Turkish model)	FTA (Canadian model)	WTO
Access to the single market	Yes	Yes	Yes	Partial	No	No	No
Have a say in the EU rule-making	Yes	No	No	No	No	No	No
Be bound by the European Court of Justice	Yes	Yes	Yes	Partial	No	No	No
Have duty-free access to the EU for goods	Yes	Yes	Yes	Yes	Yes	Yes	No
Have access to the EU market for services	Yes	Yes	Yes	Partial	No	Partial	No
Abide by the free labor mobility	Yes	Yes	Yes	Yes	No	No	No
Contribute to the EU budget	Yes	Yes	Yes	Yes	No	No	No
Be part of the EU agricultural policy	Yes	No	No	No	No	No	No
Be part of the EU commercial policy	Yes	No	No	No	Yes	No	No

Source: Own elaboration.

assume that the negotiation process between the UK and the EU will be extremely complex and lengthy, even if the UK has formally left the EU structures. Given the applicable institutional solutions, on the one hand, and the importance of the British economy for the EU, on the other hand, the stakes are undoubtedly very high.

In January 2020, the UK and the EU ratified the *Agreement on the withdrawal of the UK of Great Britain and Northern Ireland from the EU and the European Atomic Energy Community*. The content of this agreement assumes that the UK will remain a member of the Common Market until the end of 2020 to help the EU and the UK residents adapt to the new reality. After the transition period, i.e., by the end of 2020, the UK and the EU should conclude an agreement under which they will establish the final shape of their long-term relationship. If they do not conclude this agreement and do not extend the transition period, we will face a "no-deal scenario" from 2021. In the agreement signed in January, both parties declared their willingness to cooperate and to minimize Brexit-related difficulties. However, apart from declarations, it is difficult to find specific records which could lead citizens and businesses to specific legal solutions. Therefore, the negotiations in 2020 will be crucial to determine the final shape of the agreement between the EU and the UK and will probably determine the economic and social impact of Brexit on all countries concerned (Howarth & Quaglia, 2018).

Conclusions

Despite the rather complex relations between the UK and continental Europe, the former remains one of the most important members of the EU. The attitudes of Euroskepticism that have been growing there for years are not an isolated case and turn toward populist neo-nationalist movements. However, so far only the UK decided in a referendum to leave the European single market structures. There are several possible reasons for this process: political, social, economic and historical in nature. Regardless of the grounds for this decision, the future shape of the UK-EU relationship remains a significant problem. The fact that the interested parties have changed the schedule of negotiations and the date of the UK's final withdrawal from the EU several times shows how complex the views on this issue are and how difficult it is to reach a consensus. Therefore, it is crucial to prepare alternative solutions for companies that operate in times characterized by such a high degree of uncertainty.

Notes

1 In the case of Norway, the principle of free movement of goods does not cover foodstuffs, as well as regulations which stem from regional agricultural policy. For more, see Baldwin (2016).
2 It is worth to stress at this point that we can expect significant changes in the functioning of the European Economic Area. Both the European Commission and the European Council have repeatedly criticized the pace of implementation of EU regulation in three EEA member states, namely, Iceland, Liechtenstein, Norway. These organization will undoubtedly address the acknowledged imbalance in terms of benefits and obligations which result from the participation in the EEA.
3 The Council of the European Union has committed itself to reviewing relations between the EU and Switzerland and to develop detailed solutions by the end of 2018. For more, see www.consilium.europa.eu/en/press/press-releases/2017/02/28/conclusions-eu-swiss-confederation/.
4 We can illustrate this case with the RTA signed by the EU with South Korea, which gives South Korea access to the Turkish market but does not give Turkey such a right in relation to the Korean market, so the benefits are not bilateral.

References

Baldwin, R. E. (Ed.). (2016). *Brexit beckons: Thinking ahead by leading economists.* London: Centre for Economic Policy Research.

Berend, I. T. (2016). *The history of the European integration: A new perspective.* London & New York: Routledge.

Blackwell, M. (1993). *Clinging to grandeur: British attitudes and foreign policy in the aftermath of the Second World War.* London: Greenwood Press.

Corbett, S. (2016). The social consequences of Brexit for the UK and Europe. Europscepticism, populism, nationalism, and societal division. *The International Journal of Social Quality*, *9*(2), 11–31. https://doi.org/10.3167/IJSQ.2016.060102

Cowburn, A. (2016). Theresa May says "Brexit means Brexit" and there will be no attempt to remain inside the EU. *The Independent.* Retrieved August 23, 2016 from www.independent.co.uk/news/uk/politics/rocess-may-brexit-means-brexit-conservative-leadership-no-attempt-remain-inside-eu-leave-europe-a7130596.html

De Santis, R. A. (2012). The Euro area sovereign debt crisis: Safe haven, credit rating agencies and the spread of the fever from Greece, Ireland and Portugal. *ECB Working Paper Series*, 1419. Retrieved from www.ecb.europa.eu/pub/pdf/scpwps/ecbwp1419.pdf

Electoral Commission. (2016). *Results and turnout at the EU referendum*. Retrieved from www.electoralcommission.org.uk/find-information-by-subject/elections-and-referendums/past-elections-and-referendums/eu-referendum/electorate-and-count-information

European Commission. (2018). *EU expenditure and revenue*. Retrieved from http://ec.europa.eu/budget/figures/interactive/index_en.cfm

Featherstone, K. (2011). The Greek sovereign debt crisis and EMU: A failing state in a skewed regime. *Journal of Common Market Studies, 49*(2), 193–217. https://doi.org/10.1111/j.1468-5965.2010.02139.x

Frost, G. S. (2018). *The Victorian world: Facts and fictions*. Santa Barbara, CA: ABC-Clio.

Goodwin, M., & Heath, O. (2016). Brexit vote explained: Poverty, low skills and lack of opportunities. *Joseph Rowntree Foundation*. Retrieved from www.jrf.org.uk/report/brexit-vote-explained-poverty-low-skills-and-lack-opportunities

Gordon, R., & Moffatt, R. (2016). *Brexit: The immediate legal consequences*. The Constitution Society. Retrieved from https://consoc.org.uk/wp-content/uploads/2016/05/Brexit-PDF.pdf

Henderson, A., Jeffery, C., Linera, R., Scully, R., Wincott, D., & Jones, P. W. (2016). England, englishness and Brexit. *Political Quarterly, 87*(2), 187–199.

Howarth, D., & Quaglia, L. (2017). Brexit and the single European financial market. *Journal of Common Market Studies, 55*(1), 149–164.

Howarth, D., & Quaglia, L. (2018). Brexit and the battle for financial services. *Journal of European Public Policy, 25*(8), 1118–1136. https://doi.org/10.1080/13501763.2018.1467950

Kenny, M. (2016). The genesis of English nationalism. *Political Insight, 7*(2), 8–11. https://doi.org/10.1177/2041905816666124

Lane, P. R. (2012). The European sovereign debt crisis. *Journal of Economic Perspectives, 26*(3), 49–68. https://doi.org/10.1257/jep.26.3.49

Leconte, C. (2015). From pathology to mainstream phenomenon: Reviewing the Euroscepticism debate in research and theory. *International Political Science Review, 36*(3), 250–263.

Mance, H., Baker, A., & Parker, G. (2018). Brexit timeline: Key dates in the UK's divorce from EU. *Financial Times*. Retrieved from www.ft.com/content/723de327-09cb-4f0b-8b79-6ac8a4051aac

Mikołajczyk, M. (2016). Europejskie dylematy Wielkiej Brytanii. Od planu Schumana do brexitu (The European dilemmas of Great Britain. From the Schuman plan to Brexit). *Przegląd Zachodni, 4*(361), 7–35. Retrieved from https://iz.poznan.pl/plik,pobierz,1771,8c7e6211d72167e868b01d4abf3cc0f4/Marek%20Mikolajczyk,%20Europejskie%20dylematy%20Wielkiej%20Brytanii%20%E2%80%93%20od%20planu%20Schumana%20do%20Brexitu.pdf

Miller, V. (2015). *The 1974–75 UK renegotiation of EEC membership and referendum*. House of Commons Library, Briefing Paper No 7253. Retrieved from https://researchbriefings.files.parliament.uk/documents/CBP-7253/CBP-7253.pdf

Miller, V. (2016). *Brexit unknowns*. House of Commons Library Briefing Paper 7761. Retrieved from https://researchbriefings.files.parliament.uk/documents/CBP-7761/CBP-7761.pdf

Mrzygłód, U. (2010). Stanowisko Wielkiej Brytanii w kwestii euro a proces integracji rynków finansowych (The position of Great Britain on the euro and the process of financial market integration). *Acta Universitatis Lodziensis. Folia Oeconomica, 238*, 159–171. Retrieved from http://dspace.uni.lodz.pl:8080/xmlui/bitstream/handle/11089/400/159-171. pdf?sequence=1&isAllowed=y

OECD (2018). *Trade in goods and services*. Retrieved from https://data.oecd.org/trade/trade-in-goods-and-services.htm

Office for National Statistics. (2020). *Foreign direct investment involving UK companies: Outward*. Retrieved from www.ons.gov.uk/businessindustryandtrade/business/businessinnovation/datasets/foreigndirectinvestmentinvolvingukcompaniesoutwardtables

Piris, J. C. (2016). *If the UK votes to leave: The seven alternatives to EU membership*. London: Centre for European Reform.

Radwan, A. (2015). *Schuman i jego Europa (Schuman and his Europe)*. Warsaw: Biblioteka Schumana.

Rozenek, G. (2012). Wielka Brytania we wspólnotach europejskich i Unii Europejskiej (Great Britain in the European communities and the European Union). *Roczniki Nauk Społecznych, 40*(2), 101–121. Retrieved from www.kul.pl/files/852/media/RNS/pdf-y/2012/2012_2-_ronek.pdf

Startin, N. (2015). Have we reached the tipping point? The mainstreaming of Euroscepticism in the UK. *International Political Science Review, 36*(3), 311–323.

Szymczyński, T. R. (2016). Brexit a wyzwania identyfikacyjne w odniesieniu do procesu integracji europejskiej z perspektywy hermeneutycznej (Brexit and identification challenges in relation to the European integration process from the hermeneutic perspective). *Rocznik Integracji Europejskiej, 10*, 67–80. https://doi.org/10.14746/rie.2016.10.5

Walker, N. (2020). *Brexit timeline: events leading to the UK's exit from the European Union*. Briefing Paper 7960. House of Commons Library. Retrieved from https://researchbriefings.files.parliament.uk/documents/CBP-7960/CBP-7960.pdf

Wilkes, G. (1997). *Britain's failure to enter the European community 1961–1963: The enlargement negotiations and crisis in European, Atlantic and Commonwealth relations*. London: Frank Cass.

Woś, J. (2001). Rynek i państwo w modelach współczesnej gospodarki rynkowej (The market and the state in the models of the modern market economy). *Ruch Prawniczy, Ekonomiczny i Socjologiczny, 63*(4), 173–191. Retrieved from https://repozytorium.amu.edu.pl/bitstream/10593/5163/1/10_Jerzy_Wos_Rynek%20i%20pa%C5%84stwo%20w%20modelach%20wsp%C3%B3%C5%82czesnej%20gospodarki_173-191.pdf

3 The projected effects of Brexit on the EU and the UK[1]

Marian Gorynia, Aleksandra Kania,
Ewa Mińska-Struzik

Introduction

The origins of Brexit presented in Chapter 2 lead to a broader reflection, which boils down to the following questions:

- What were the tendencies in international economic relations in the second half of the twentieth century and in the twenty-first century?
- Do these tendencies continue and are likely to continue, or do we face a period of re-evaluations and peculiar twists and turns?
- What are the fundamental challenges for humanity due to globalization regardless of Brexit and what impact can Brexit have on them?
- In what sense do contemporary processes form the Brexit's basis and context? What does Brexit change in these tendencies?

This subchapter attempts to answer these questions.

The UK's decision to leave the EU was a landmark moment for European integration. The British electorate voted to leave the EU by a 51.9% majority. The result of the referendum on Brexit organized on June 23, 2016, surprised many observers and started a series of attempts to anticipate what the consequences would be for both the British and European economies. Several institutions published model-based forecasts on the economic consequences of Brexit, including the OECD, Oxford Economics, the Centre for Economic Performance, PricewaterhouseCoopers (PwC) and HM Treasury. Some experts, such as those from PwC, predict a slight negative impact of Brexit on British GDP, which equals 1.3% in the short term. Others, such as the researchers from the Centre for Economic Performance, predict a significant fall in British GDP in the long run, which equals 9.3%. All these institutions adopted two assumptions for the UK's relations with the EU after Brexit. First, the UK would make a zero or lower contribution to the EU budget, depending on the state's access to markets. Second, trade relations between the UK and the EU would change (Armstrong, 2016).

The selected Brexit projections we will present in this chapter represent two potential scenarios for the UK's trade relations with the EU, namely the "soft" and "hard" Brexit. The "hard" Brexit presupposes the absence of trade agreements between the UK and the EU. In such a scenario, the WTO would determine the trade rules. The "soft" Brexit assumes that the UK and the EU member states would sign complex-free trade agreements, which include not only customs duties but also low costs of NTBs to trade (Felbermayr, Fuest, Gröschl, & Stöhlker, 2017). Experts predict that the average effects will be negative in both scenarios, but more negative consequences for the British and European economies may occur in the case of "hard" Brexit (Dhingra, Machin, & Overman, 2017). In this chapter, we will review selected results of research on Brexit effects for the EU and the UK economies. The studies we will present are based on various methods and assumptions to analyze several aspects of Brexit: from potential changes in GDP and price levels through trade and immigration to foreign investment. These studies try to answer how Europe will change in the next few years because of the decision made by the British.

Globalization and integration processes: significance for modern Europe

We should pay attention to the most important process in the whole post-war period, namely the development of international economic cooperation. This process had different pace in various parts of the world, but the general trend has been clear. We may call this process the internationalization of economic activity. It means the development of economic links between different sectors of the world economy, at the micro level – the increasing number of companies engaged in cooperation with foreign countries, and at the macro level, the participation of national economies in this cooperation. However, we should stress that internationalization processes immediately after the Second World War showed a low level of intensity. In general, it was not until the 1970s and 1980s that there was a rapid increase in internationalization processes. The main – but not the only – manifestations of economic cooperation internationalization are international trade and FDI. Experts refer to the process that counteracts internationalization as reverse internationalization. While researchers use the former term in both the macro and micro contexts – i.e., either in the internationalization of a country's economy or in the internationalization of a company – the literature usually employs the latter in the context of enterprises.

We may characterize globalization as the rapid increase in the scope of aforementioned links combined with their high intensity, i.e., the increase in the number of cooperating units and the scale of cooperation between these units. Therefore, we should treat globalization as a higher, more advanced stage of internationalization. On the other hand, experts usually define deglobalization as the reverse process, i.e., a decrease in the scope and intensity of links between entities involved in international economic cooperation. We should foreground here the complex issues of defining these matters and highlight the ambiguity and multidimensionality of the concept of globalization (e.g., see Bhagwati, 2004; Brown, 1992; Dicken, 1998; Dunning, 2003; Gilpin, 2000;

Gorynia, 2002; Milward, 2003; Nederveen, 2012; Ohmae, 1995; Parker, 1998; Rodrik, 2011; Stiglitz, 2002, 2011; Streeten, 1998; Stiglitz, 2008). McCann (2018, p. 6) concludes that it is pointless to seek a definition that will satisfy everyone. It would be unreasonable to reduce the globalization process solely to its economic dimension. Kowalski (2013, p. 13) interestingly describes the social sciences approach to globalization aspects and identifies the following disciplines that study globalization: sociology, economics, cultural studies, political science, international relations and development economics. We assume for this study that globalization is the highest stage of internationalization of multidimensional relationships among different countries in terms of intensity. Various analyses and approaches to globalization in the literature on the subject differ in the distribution of emphasis. Later, we will present the concepts of several authors, selected for their intellectual contributions that allow for an interdisciplinary explanation and understanding of globalization processes. However, we mainly focus here on the economic aspects of globalization.

We may define globalization in the economic sphere as a process of gradual blurring of borders between individual national economies, expressed by the intensification of international trade flows and the increased migration of capital, people and technology (cf. Primo Braga, 2017, p. 30). As we focus on the economic perspective, we should foreground that scholars sometimes reduce globalization to the microeconomic dimension, in which the behavior of multinational corporations (MNEs) plays the primary role. These corporations want to achieve a total presence in all (or most) markets and a far-reaching standardization of activities in those markets (Yip, 1995, 2001). The increase in the scope and intensity of economic relations can proceed according to two model solutions. The first solution implies a relatively steady increase in the importance of international cooperation between all countries, which is internationalization and dispersed – or evenly distributed – globalization. The second solution involves a significant diversification of the importance of international economic cooperation with different groups of countries, which is regionalization. Thus, we may understand regionalization as a differentiation of the nature and intensity of economic cooperation concerning different groups of countries separated by geographical criterion with a tendency to focus on one or more groups of countries. In turn, the reverse process is unitarization, which means a reversal of regionalization trends toward the universality of principles and the intensity of cooperation with all countries of the world.

International economic integration can be as a specific case of regionalization. The essence of international economic integration lies in the increased intensity of economic links within the group of countries that form an integrational organization. We may understand regionalization as a middle way to deepen internationalization and globalization. That is, the period of regional cooperation development usually precedes opening to cooperation with the "rest of the world". In this light, we may perceive regional economic cooperation agreements – or integration agreements – as an intermediate step toward the globalization of the world economy. Kołodko (2013, pp. 190–211) provides numerous arguments to justify such a viewpoint: "regional integration is an opportunity not only to intensify pro-development cooperation in the region but also to improve institutional and political coordination on a global scale" (Kołodko, 2013, p. 190). The question remains as to how the concepts of regionalization and economic integration relate to each other. The first solution is to assume that regionalization equals integration. Most scholars agree that integration means the intensification of economic cooperation with a specific group of countries, while relationships with other countries are less intense and subject to different rules. However, it seems that in the case of integration, there is an additional requirement for higher degree institutionalization and formalization of economic links, despite similarities to economic regionalization. Therefore, the scholarship assumes that regionalization means the unique nature of cooperation within a specific group of countries that belong to a specific geographical region. In turn, integration is a special case of regionalization, characterized by the high institutionalization and formalization of economic cooperation within the group of countries that form an integration community. As a result, we may assume that disintegration will be a process of withdrawal from adopted integration agreements, which will mean that economic cooperation among countries that belong to an integration group will weaken.

Possible analytical approaches – or levels of process analysis – are another important aspect of globalization. Typically, scholars distinguish three primary levels of analysis: macro, meso and micro (Gorynia & Kowalski, 2008; Kowalski, 2013, pp. 20–25). The first level focuses on the national economies of countries involved in globalization processes. The analyses of the meso level focus on the industry and sector dimension of globalization. Scholars apply the micro level to the behavior of enterprises engaged in globalization processes. Similarly, we may build a typology of analytical approaches to internationalization, reverse internationalization, regionalization, unitarization, integration and disintegration.

We should also pay attention to globalization periodization. As Michie (2017, p. 27) indicates, globalization is nothing new: it is globalization's modern form that is new. Researchers usually assume that the first wave of globalization occurred in 1870–1914, when governments widely abandoned protectionist measures and liberalized trade, which led to the increase in the volume of international trade (cf. Ziewiec, 2012). The second wave of globalization happened in 1950–1970, when the world governments built the foundations of institutional reglobalization, which we may characterize as a return to the first-wave globalization. The process involved the creation of such international economic and political organizations as the United Nations, the International Monetary Fund, the World Bank and the General Agreement on Tariffs and Trade. Moreover, the second wave involved the initial rise in the importance of international corporations. The third wave began in the 1980s and included the development of communication technologies and financial markets, along with large shifts in worldwide production activities. Scholars still disagree on the interpretation of the turmoil in international economic cooperation in the context of the 2008–2011 global economic crisis. Neither did they develop a shared view on the changes in economic relations caused by US policy during President Donald Trump's term in office. We may only assume that the decline in globalization trends that we face in the second decade of the twenty-first century may prove to be the predecessor of the next, fourth phase of globalization.

Causes, manifestations and effects of globalization

Most authors agree that the measure of internationalization and globalization may be the degree of the liberalization of economic relations among countries or groups of countries. We must indicate that this degree at the international level is a prerequisite for deepening internationalization and globalization processes. However, this does not mean that we distinguished all the necessary conditions for these processes to occur. It appears that the primary and most important foundations of globalization involve two circumstances: the global primacy of market economy principles and broad scientific-technological progress. Despite many weaknesses, the market economy is the most efficient social and economic system in humanity's history in terms of its ability to ensure the welfare of societies. The *"homo economicus"* stereotype turned out to be the flywheel of economic development and, more broadly, of civilizational progress. Only in such regulatory conditions could dynamic scientific and technical progress become a true catalyst for change in the real economy; in terms of production, sales and infrastructure, mainly communications and transport. In fact, modern technologies pressure the broad global commercialization of products, as they aim to maximize profits. These modern technologies increase the productivity of machines and equipment and make cargo transportation cheaper and more reliable. In turn, advances in information and communication technologies improve the search for recipients and suppliers abroad. From a technical and managerial viewpoint, the geographical diversification of individual links in the value chain has become not only possible but also desirable due to diversified levels of capital and labor intensity and differences in the cost of these resources (cf. Gorynia & Mińska-Struzik, 2018). Other prerequisites required for the occurrence of the signaled processes are, e.g., world peace, transportation systems safety and reliability of the international settlement system (cf. Kowalski, 2013, p. 17). Only the cumulative fulfilment of these conditions can lay the foundations for internationalization and globalization. Therefore, we should emphasize that only cooperation in the regulatory sphere and real economy could have led to such spectacular results in terms of internationalization and economic globalization.

Some publications assess globalization in terms of opportunities and threats. Streeten (1998, p. 30) proposes a concept of the balance sheet of globalization in which he identifies those who benefited from globalization and those who lost. The voice of economists is also essential in the debate between supporters and opponents of globalization. The approach of Bhagwati (2004) is an example of a factual and reliable analysis of the issue. Bhagwati identifies the advantages and disadvantages of globalization in the following arrangement:

poverty – reduction – increase; child labor – reduction – increase; the role of women – improvement – regress; democracy – promotion – reduction; culture – enrichment – endangerment; wages and labor standards – increase – decrease; environment – improvement – deterioration; MNEs – useful agents – predators; crime – decrease – increase; health – improvement – regress.

We should also pay attention to Orłowski's (2016, p. 217) take on the matter. In general, he agrees with Kołodko (2013) that "on a global scale, the balance of globalization is beneficial". At the same time, Orłowski indicates that globalization also causes many controversies. He presents five major faults of globalization posited by its critics (Stiglitz, 2002). These controversies include unfair rules of the game, imposed by stronger developed countries, and the focus of globalization processes exclusively on profit and tangible assets, with disregard for all other aspects of life. Moreover, Orłowski includes such issues as undemocratic restrictions on the sovereignty of many developing countries and unequal distribution of globalization's benefits. Finally, these controversies include the imposition of an unsuitable economic system on many developing countries, unsuitable to their traditions, cultures, and developmental challenges.

Moreover, we should note the views of Rodrik (2011), who approaches globalization in an interdisciplinary way to highlight the conflicts between democracy, the interests of nation-states and economic globalization. Moreover, he suggests how to resolve them. The same author (Rodrik, 2018) notes that there are many empirical studies in the literature on the subject, which demonstrate links between the emergence of populist movements and forces associated with globalization. We can illustrate the former with Donald Trump and right-wing Republicans in the United States, Brexit in the UK and extreme right-wing groups across Europe. The examples of the latter include terms of trade shocks with China, increasing import penetration levels, deindustrialization and immigration. With Brexit, scholars indicate that the significant increase in immigration processes in the UK increased the number of people who voted for Brexit (Becker, Fetzer, & Novy, 2017). Furthermore, Colantone and Stanig (2018) found that in regions of the UK with a higher import penetration rate from China, the percentage of pro-Brexit voters also was higher.

Summarizing the above and the extensive literature on globalization, we may distinguish four elementary attitudes:

- enthusiasm (slightly cooled by reason): pro-, affirmation (but not blind; e.g., Bhagwati, 2004);
- moderate reflection: medium, balance (e.g., Streeten, 1998);
- mistrust: a critical approach but without full negation (e.g., Stiglitz, 2004, 2008; Szymański, 2007); and
- questioning the importance of and postulating a retreat from globalization, which leads to reverse globalization: Donald Trump and similar leaders, new protectionism and new nationalism (Kołodko & Koźmiński, 2017).

Brexit belongs to the last attitude.

The future of globalization

Reflection on globalization's future should refer to both spheres of the socio-economic system – the real economy and the regulatory sphere – just as the diagnosis of its causes, manifestations and effects refers to these spheres. It seems that the elementary development trend in the real economy in the predictable future will be the continuation in global prosperity level improvement process. Obviously, this view raises many doubts about the measurement of welfare, the distribution of wealth among groups of countries, among countries and within countries. In comparison with humanity's demographic development, the environment's eco-efficiency will be an essential condition for the manifestation of the signaled trend. However, it is unlikely that all possible conditions will undermine the impact of broadly defined scientific and technological progress. Therefore, scientific and technological progress will most likely become the dominant trend in the real global economy. We can even legitimately apply this trend a status close to the law of nature. However, we do not know what parameters will characterize the appearance of this law: the rate of scientific-technical progress and its global distribution. We may assume that if the pace of innovation growth is high, there will appear intense pressure to commercialize these innovations as widely as possible. This process would be a driving force behind economic globalization. The likely persistence of low growth rates in innovation will work in the opposite direction: globalization impulses will then weaken. After all, only products created as a result of innovative activity are subject to commercial diffusion on a global scale.

However, innovation processes do not happen in a vacuum, and the interaction between the real economy and the regulatory sphere will be significant, given the differences between the two groups of countries: the developed and the developing countries. We should discuss here the interesting views of Gomułka (2016). He offers valuable insights regarding the prospects for long- and medium-term global economic growth, which lead to the outline of three highly probable trends as follows:

• Technological and institutional changes will be the key determinants of systematic economic growth. The importance of the latter may be fundamental as they affect the former.
• The mechanisms and results of technological changes differ between developed countries – which form the so-called World Technology Frontier (the WTF sphere) – and developing economies. In the former, the most important are first-generation innovations, which determine the changes in quality. What generates these changes are expenditures on the R&D sector and education. Both rates tend to be stable and hardly depend on differences in national economic policies and national institutional changes. As a result, GDP growth rates in developed countries are similar. The situation in the developing countries is different as the innovation rate depends mainly on the transfer and absorption of innovation accumulated in the

past in the WTF sphere. In turn, these processes result from investment in fixed capital and human capital's support. What is important here are each country's institutions and economic policies. Usually, the innovation rate in these countries is relatively high due to transfers of innovation from the WTF. Still, the rate tends to decline due to a decrease in transfer possibilities. Besides, the economic growth rate of each developing country also slows down over time.

- Therefore, we may conclude that we require two different theories to explain global growth processes; one refers to the WTF countries and the other to developing countries. The implications of the two theories for prediction building are different. The role of institutions is crucial in this respect, as they can facilitate innovation transfer. Thus, institutions influence growth rates, especially in developing countries.

We should highlight another important circumstance: the conditions of globalization processes on the regulatory side. It seems that in the foreseeable future, the world's prevailing socioeconomic system will be market-based capitalism, while the number of its possible variations will change (increase), defined especially by the scope and nature of the role played by the state. To a large extent, the prevailing regulatory system is a consequence of the state's importance. The roles adopted by individual states will be the primary determinant of the relationship between the regulatory sphere and globalization. If a liberal attitude prevails around the world, we may expect a return to the globalization trends developed at the turn of the second and third millennium. If anti-liberal attitudes dominate the global scene, the period return to the said globalization trends may take longer. This return will occur anyway because of the immanent characteristics of market economy.

The global approach to populist trends will also be of great importance for the future of globalization. Rodrik (2018) drafts three possible scenarios in this respect:

- Bad: a situation similar to the 1930s, when global economic cooperation collapsed, and strongly right-wing and strongly left-wing regimes emerged;
- Ugly: creeping populism and protectionism will damage both liberal democracy and an open global economy; and
- Good: a democratic restoration of balance will result in the abandonment of hyper-globalization ideas and the restoration of a greater amount of autonomy to nations.

According to Rodrik (2018), the restoration of balance in the "good" scenario should mainly concern the following directions: from capital and business to labor and the rest of society; from global governance to national governance; from areas where the economic benefits of globalization are small to areas where they are significant.

The Polish literature discusses globalization within assessment of the new pragmatism theory (Gorynia, 2017a, 2017b; Kołodko, 2014). The tendency to associate or even identify new pragmatism as globalization is striking. One may worry that this identification is confusing, misleading and may cause a terminological commotion. As we indicated earlier, the economic approach allows treating globalization as a process of increasing economic links among countries. In this view, globalization simply means the progressive development of economic cooperation. For the process of globalization to occur, it is necessary to respect the principle of freedom to do business internationally and, more specifically, globally. In this sense, globalization is very similar to the liberalization of economic relations among countries. Thus, as Koźmiński equalizes new pragmatism with globalization, he comes close to the conclusion that new pragmatism is related to liberalization, which is not far from liberalism. Knowing Kołodko's perspective, we may suppose he would disagree with such a logical interpretation of the relationship between globalization and new pragmatism. It is hard to imagine Kołodko accepting the conclusion that the new pragmatism he advocates implies liberalism, which after all, implies a relatively small role of state intervention in the economy. In fact, an additional and difficult dilemma arises here: is it liberalism that drives globalization or globalization processes force the increasing liberalization of international economic relations? Moreover, the question arises whether we may reconcile the affirmation of globalization and the condemnation of neoliberalism? Perhaps the recipe for reconciliation of these discrepancies would be to establish a "world government?" However, Rodrik (2011) seems to answer the last question by introducing the notion of "globalization paradox," meaning that one cannot have three things at the same time: globalization, democracy and the nation-state.

Moreover, we should consider one more circumstance that determines the future of globalization processes at the junction of real economy and regulatory sphere. This circumstance is the future of international economic cooperation in the context of the ongoing Fourth Industrial Revolution (Industry 4.0). The literature on the subject highlights that "currently, global information flows generate more value than traditional trade in goods" (Manyika et al., 2016). Therefore, we should not focus on declining flows of capital or stagnating trade as evidence against globalization. Instead, we should acknowledge that globalization enters a new phase, defined by mass flows of information (Götz, 2018). Indeed, these circumstances can cause some difficulties in the perception, description, measurement and analysis of globalization. However, we should not exaggerate or overestimate these circumstances: in the market economy, we generally deal with payments alongside the supply of goods, services or information. Interested parties pay through banking systems. The systems are subject to the tax authorities' scrutiny and finally reflected in the international statistics. From this viewpoint, it is of little importance whether we pay for oil supplies or databases.

In light of the above, we should also note Kołodko's (2013) remarks on the challenges that humanity faces in globalization processes. He presents these processes as a dozen "great future issues": the pace and limits of economic growth; the evolution of values and their cultural implications for development processes; the institutionalization of globalization; the growing lack of coordination that leads to chaos; regional integration and its link to globalization; the position and role of NGOs; the environment and competition for finite natural resources; demographic processes; the migration of population; poverty, misery, and social inequalities; knowledge-based economy and society; scientific and technological progress; evolution of the Internet and its economic consequences; conflicts, security, war and peace.

Finally, we should return to the elementary question of globalization's future and its relationship with Brexit. First, market economy domination seems the most probable in the world's foreseeable future, along with the tendency to evolutionarily continue globalization as its immanent feature, which allows modifications of its current course. The number of countries that will not be market economies is unlikely to grow, but it does not seem that there are any exceptions from the indicated pattern of market regulation supremacy. Therefore, the literal "end of history" will not happen but will become a directional trend in world history, which will see the functioning of a significant number of capitalist economy variations. However, in the long run, globalization does not seem reversible.

Second, the process of globalization is a process that will never end. There will be periods of intensification and deceleration of globalization processes. There will even be periods of deglobalization, but complete globalization will never happen (Kołodko, 2013, p. 107). Globalization will evolve, change and mature. This scenario is based on the belief that the benefits of globalization are greater than its disadvantages. What is Brexit and what will it be if we perceive at globalization from the above perspective? What is Brexit in the context of the outlined theoretical approaches? In terms of the long-term perspective, we can reduce Brexit to an episode, a deviation from the general pattern.

Brexit is one of the numerous examples of actions and events that influenced the evolution of globalization in the past and will influence it in the future. Kołodko (2013, p. 108) writes that "in 1914–1988, there were many indications that globalization retreats, whereas these were only temporary, albeit three-generational, economic frictions in its incessant push forward". We can link other possible and non-excludable future disruptions to the globalization, e.g., to the possible outbreak of the Israeli-Iranian or Sino-Taiwanese conflict. This broad perspective raises the question of what may happen in the future with UK's membership in the EU and the international economic community. Is Brexit reversible? Will "Bre-entry" seem possible in the future? It is difficult to give a definitive answer to these questions today.

As far as we consider Brexit's influence on globalization processes, Britain's withdrawal from the EU is undoubtedly a sign of deglobalization. By its very nature, Brexit is an example of the spread of populist tendencies and it is not an isolated case. In the economic perspective, the basic demands of Brexit aim to strengthen protectionism and limit economic freedom in international cooperation. In short- and mid-term, Brexit will have noticeable negative economic consequences that will spread differently in different regions and sectors, particularly in relations with the EU member states. However, from a long-term viewpoint and the perspective of the global economy, the economic significance of Brexit will nonetheless be moderate. Therefore, it will not significantly affect globalization tendencies.

Another observation is related to the synergy of regional integration and globalization processes, which we previously mentioned in the context of Kołodko's works. From this viewpoint, Brexit is a violation of integration tendencies, a fracture on their map and an example of a step toward disintegration. Therefore, we should perceive Brexit as a sign of deglobalization also in this context.

The projected effects of Brexit on the UK

The result of the referendum became clear on the night of June 23–24, 2016. Immediately after, the British pound suffered a sharp drop against the US dollar and the euro. The downtrend continued in the following months and, until November 2017, the British pound's value was still about 10% lower than before the referendum (Breinlich, Leromain, Novy, & Sampson, 2017). The reaction of the British currency exchange rate was a clear signal that deglobalization will be costly first and foremost for those who initiated the process. Manifested in the depreciation of the exchange rate of the British pound, the retreat from globalization – according to economic theory – induced further changes in the condition of British economy's parameters.

Economic theory predicts that a prolonged and robust depreciation of the exchange rate in a country should increase inflation through increased import costs. In fact, the UK's Consumer Inflation Index (CPI) rose from 0.5% in June 2016 to 2.6% in June 2017 and then to 3.0% in September 2017. Researchers observed a positive correlation between import exposure and price increases after the referendum. In the year following the referendum, the referendum shock led to a rise in total inflation in the UK by 1.7 percentage points (Breinlich et al., 2017).[2]

These immediately visible effects of Brexit were due to the UK economy's significant dependence on the EU. The UK is more dependent on the EU than the other way around. Even 12.6% of the UK's GDP is linked to exports to the EU, while only 3.1% of other EU member states' GDP is linked to exports to the UK. The EU is the destination for 44% of UK exports, and 60% of total trade in the UK depends on EU membership, including preferential access to 53 markets outside the EU that the membership provided. Moreover, the UK is a service economy: the service sector accounts for almost 80% of the country's economy. Although the UK has a net trade deficit with the EU, in 2013, it recorded a net services surplus of £10.3 billion. With 36% of total British exports of services, the EU was one of its largest partners (European Movement International, 2017).

The UK is also the leading location for EU FDIs, as it combines an English-speaking and relatively flexible labor market with barrier-free access to the EU single market. Market size is the primary determinant of the volume of FDI flows, and EU membership has expanded the UK market. Barriers that matter to investors in a competitive modern economy are not tariffs, but NTBs such as differing national standards and regulations. The EU single market provided a level playing field, as it replaced 28 sets of regulations with a single rule book and allowed companies free access to 500 million customers who work with them. After Brexit, the UK is likely to lose full access to the single market, which will make the country less attractive for companies that would like to use the UK as a base for their investments in the EU market (European Movement International, 2017).

The Oxford Economics team (2016) conducted a comprehensive study on the projected impact of Brexit on the UK. Their study analyzed nine scenarios for trade relations between the UK and the EU after Brexit. The scenarios consider the impact of regulatory, migration and fiscal policy choices on economic conditions. The results are based on the Oxford Economics' Global Economic Model. In the best-case scenario of an EU-like membership (customs union with the EU and high level of integration), real GDP in 2030 would amount to only 0.1%. less than if Brexit had not happened. In the worst-case scenario with no free trade UK-EU agreement, the emergence of "populist" measures such as immigration control, and no liberalization of regulations, the British real GDP will fall by 3.9% by 2030. Most scenarios impose significant long-term costs on the UK economy. However, the Oxford Economics team describes even the worst-case scenarios as "far from disastrous". The authors indicate that the UK government can reduce potential economic costs if it adopts liberal economic policies such as deregulation, tax cuts and limited restrictions on immigration.

The British think tank Open Europe published another important and very detailed analysis of Brexit's effects (Booth, Howarth, Persson, Ruparel, & Swidli, 2015). The study used the computable general equilibrium (CGE) trading model to estimate the ex-ante Brexit effects. According to the researchers, in the worst-case scenario, the UK will not negotiate a preferential trade agreement with the EU, so that new trade barriers will affect British companies' access to the EU. FTAs with third countries will remain in force, and the UK's annual net contribution to the EU budget will be saved. Nevertheless, this scenario leads to a permanent loss of 2.2% of British GDP. The study also mentions the significant risk that – after Brexit – the UK government may increase business costs and weaken competitiveness by implementing an interventionist policy.

In turn, Ottaviano, Pessoa, Sampson, and Reenen (2014) propose two scenarios for the development of the UK after Brexit – optimistic and pessimistic – which they developed based on the gravity model of international trade.[3] In the optimistic scenario, the UK will negotiate an agreement with the EU, just as Switzerland and Norway did. As a result, tariffs will continue to be zero, and NTBs will represent a quarter of the reduceable NTBs faced by US exporters to

Table 3.1 Scenarios for the post-Brexit development of the UK

Scenario		Comment
Optimistic scenario		
Welfare change due to increase in EU/UK tradable tariffs	0%	No tariffs imposed
Welfare change due to increase in EU/UK non-tariffs barriers	−0.4%	Slight increase
Welfare change due to future falls in EU/UK NTBs	−1.26%	–
Welfare change due to fiscal benefit	0.53%	–
Total welfare change	−1.13%	–
Pessimistic scenario		
Welfare change due to increase in EU/UK tradable tariffs	−0.14%	MFN EU tariffs
Welfare change due to increase in EU/UK non-tariffs barriers	−0.93%	Moderate increase
Welfare change due to future falls in EU/UK NTBs	−2.55%	–
Welfare change due to fiscal benefit	0.53%	–
Total welfare change	−3.09%	–

Source: Own elaboration based on Ottaviano et al. (2014, p. 8).

Table 3.2 Brexit impact on the employment level in the UK (the number of persons)

	2020		2025		2030	
soft Brexit	−550,000	−1.7%	−450,000	−1.4%	−350,000	−1.1%
hard Brexit	−950,000	−2.9%	−950,000	−2.9%	−600,000	−1.8%

Source: Own elaboration based on PricewaterhouseCoopers (2016).

the EU. In a pessimistic scenario, the UK will be unable to negotiate favorable conditions with the EU, and the costs of trade will increase significantly. In both scenarios, the main potential benefit of Brexit for the UK is the net saved contribution to the EU budget of 0.53% of GDP. Possible negative effects include a decline in British GDP. In the optimistic case, the UK's GDP level will fall by 1.1%; in the pessimistic case, it will fall by 3.1% in the longer term (Table 3.1).

The study results of the European Movement International (2017) – the largest pan-European network of pro-European organizations – are consistent with the above. EMI's most optimistic scenarios predict 2.2% losses of British GDP. In the absolute best-case scenario, the UK would benefit from leaving Europe: with a 1.6% higher GDP in 2030. PricewaterhouseCoopers (2016) examined changes in employment levels (Table 3.2) and GDP per capita (Table 3.3) in the post-Brexit UK in different time horizons.

They show that both "soft" and "hard" Brexit can lead to a significant fall in the UK's employment rates, with the most severe changes to take place in the short term, i.e., by 2020. We can observe a similar relationship in research results of GDP per capita: the British society's wealth will fall the most within the first few years after the pessimistic scenario becomes a reality.

Table 3.3 Brexit impact on GDP

Dimension	2020			2025			2030		
	soft	*hard*	*diff*	*soft*	*hard*	*diff*	*soft*	*hard*	*diff*
Uncertainty	−1.9	−2.6	−0.7	−0.1	−0.9	−0.8	−0.1	−0.1	0
Trade	−0.5	−1.7	−1.2	−0.5	−1.9	−1.4	−0.5	−2.1	−1.6
Migration	−0.8	−1.3	−0.5	−0.8	−1.6	−0.8	−1.0	−1.6	−0.6
Regulations	0.0	0.0	0	0.3	0.3	0	0.3	0.3	0
Fiscal	0.1	0.1	0	0.0	0.0	0	0.0	0.0	0
Total impact on GDP	−3.1	−5.5	−2.4	−1.1	−4.1	−3.0	−1.2	−3.5	−2.3
Total impact on GDP *per capita*	−3.0	−5.4	−2.4	−0.9	−3.6	−2.7	−0.8	−2.7	−1.9

Source: Own elaboration based on PricewaterhouseCoopers (2016).

Note: The impact is understood as UK real GDP per cent difference to counterfactual levels.

In turn, HM Treasury (2016) estimates that British GDP will fall by 7.5% within 15 years following hard Brexit and by 3.8% in the case of soft Brexit. The HM Treasury analysis utilizes a widely accepted approach to gravitational modeling, which distinguishes the specific effect of EU membership from alternative factors that affect trade and FDI. These estimates are based on EU development data from 2016, with no assumptions that further reforms will occur. Therefore, the total cost of Brexit may be higher. The introduction of an ambitious economic reform plan for the EU could contribute up to 4% to the UK's GDP – £2,800 for every household in the UK – if the EU emphasizes the reduction of remaining barriers to trade in services, energy and digital technology. For the UK outside the EU, these economic reforms would be less likely. Therefore, the cost of Brexit would be accordingly higher in terms of potential GDP loss.

The most recent analysis by the Centre for Economic Performance (Dhingra & Sampson, 2019) indicates that there is a possibility of tangible change for the UK population depending on the adopted scenario (see Table 3.4).

In each case, the researchers reported the expected impact of Brexit on the UK's per capita income 10 years after the agreement's implementation, in comparison with the alternative scenario in which the UK remains in the EU. The estimates in Table 3.4 do not consider the impact of Brexit on the UK-EU fiscal transfers or the possible benefits for the UK from new FTAs with non-EU countries. However, even under optimistic assumptions, these effects would be much lower than the costs presented in Table 3.4. The UK was a net contributor to the EU budget, but the fiscal savings from Brexit are likely to represent 0.3% of the UK's income at most (Dhingra & Sampson, 2019).

We observe similar results in a study conducted by a group of analysts from the Bundesbank, Banque de France and Banco de España (Berthou et al., 2019). Their joint study highlights some of the numerous channels through which Brexit will influence the UK economy and its economic partners. Their study

Table 3.4 Brexit impact on the income of the UK citizen

	Change in UK resident income (in comparison to staying in the EU)	
	%	Pounds
Soft Brexit – the Norwegian option	−1.6	−£500
Theresa May's scenario – customs union	−1.7	−£500
Boris Johnson's scenario – free trade agreement	−2.5	−£800
hard Brexit – WTO rules	−3.3	−£1000

Source: Own elaboration based on Bevington et al. (2019, p. 7) and Dhingra and Sampson (2019, p. 26).

Note: Values calculated at 2018 rates; the authors assume that economic models are an imperfect map of the world. The presented model was created without knowing exactly what form future relations will take and without taking into account changes in FDI, which will also shape the economic effects of Brexit. There is already some evidence that the reduction in investment flows is adversely affecting the UK economy. The CEP model also does not allow mapping the dynamic impact of trade on productivity. Trade integration can increase productivity by increasing competition, stimulating innovation or reducing the costs of intermediate goods. Therefore, the real impact of Brexit on the incomes of UK residents may be bigger.

especially focuses on trade and migration channels, with the addition of a more general assessment of the UK's withdrawal from the EU by means of the gravity model of international trade. In the medium term, the trade channel alone may reduce British GDP by 2%, if the UK returns to WTO rules. By contrast, a more general gravity model indicates a fall in British GDP by almost 6% compared to what the country could achieve if it remained in the EU. Therefore, according to the conducted analysis, the "cost of lack of Europe" would amount to 2–6% of actual losses to British GDP. Interestingly, the study also shows that the results are sensitive to the anticipated political response. We should bear in mind the conclusion that, in principle, monetary and fiscal policy can ease the shock caused by Brexit.

Noteworthy, the above static theoretical ex-ante models cover only a limited range of possible economic effects. Experts use these models to estimate the Brexit impact on the UK economy. Most of these models are based on a theoretical framework of perfectly competitive markets, in which prices only cover costs and there are no lasting profits. However, the reality is that markets are often imperfectly competitive, namely companies that differentiate their goods can charge prices above their costs. Higher international competition can lead to lower margins in favor of consumers. Therefore, reliance on perfect competition excludes the important benefits of economic integration, which are particularly relevant for trade between industrialized countries. In fact, higher international competition reduces margins and increases efficiency in companies. In turn, these processes lead to lower prices and an increase in consumers' real income.

Potentially, higher trade barriers in the EU will encourage British companies to relocate production from the UK to the EU, which is an additional potential effect which the experts did not include in the above models. Besides, increased transaction costs and delays due to customs controls – which particularly hinder trade in semi-finished products – may separate the British companies from trans-border value chains in Europe. Moreover, the UK's position as a continental foothold for non-European companies may suffer. Companies from third countries, especially the United States, use the UK as a gateway to continental Europe as they can benefit from free access to the EU internal market. The City of London's position as a center for euro-denominated financial services also remains uncertain. It seems unlikely that the European Central Bank will maintain the status quo on this issue. Moreover, the presented estimates do not consider any short-term effects, such as the costs of the economy's adjustment to new customs arrangements.

Let us emphasize that the above projections on how Brexit will affect the British economic growth depend on four factors:

- Whether the EU will implement reforms itself?
- What will be the outcome of trade agreements negotiated by the EU?
- To what extent the UK is ready to transform itself into a highly deregulated free market economy?
- What kind of relationship the UK decides to have with the EU single market?

The projected effects of Brexit on the EU

While the role of Brexit for the British economy remains important, it will have an equally noteworthy impact on EU member states' economies. The implications for trade between the EU and the UK will depend on the post-Brexit relationship between interested parties. The costs of trade between the UK and the EU will increase in both most likely scenarios, i.e., either a comprehensive free trade agreement or restriction to WTO rules. According to the Oxford Economics study, the hard Brexit may result in a 2% decline in British GDP, which is equivalent to about £40 billion (*The Economist*, 2017). These figures are much larger compared to other EU countries (see: Figure 3.1).

Studies conducted by PricewaterhouseCoopers (2016)[4] highlight the importance of Brexit for global trade. Most likely, Brexit will reduce bilateral UK-EU trade. We may directly link the volume of losses to the post-Brexit trade agreement between the EU and the UK. If trade between the EU and the UK were to return to WTO rules, by 2030, the other EU-27 countries would suffer a 0.8% reduction in their GDP. The losses caused by the FTA scenario are likely to be less severe, which would also depend on the agreement's details: the UK would experience a 3.4% decline in GDP, compared to a 0.6% fall in the EU-27 countries by 2030.

Moreover, experts from PricewaterhouseCoopers (2016) claim that Brexit will affect some sectors of the economy more than other. The industries that may experience the greatest impact on exports include automotive, electronics

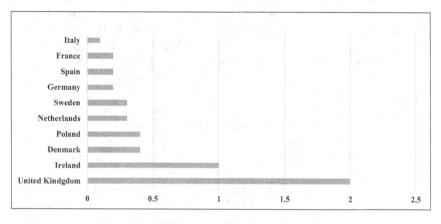

Figure 3.1 Brexit effects: GDP declines (%) in selected EU countries

Source: Own elaboration based on The Economist (2017).

and food-processing industries. Motor vehicles distinguish themselves as a commodity with the largest share of trade between the UK and the EU, as the UK is an important producer of motor vehicles and parts. Moreover, the country is an important vehicle sales market: in Europe, the UK is second only to Germany. In turn, the EU is the UK's primary export market, as the EU received 57.5% of British vehicle exports. If the UK and the EU fail to negotiate a free trade agreement, then the customs duty rate for cars could amount to 10% (European Movement International, 2017). Noteworthy, some sectors perform better in each scenario, even when aggregate GDP falls: e.g., the financial sector in some EU member states or the agricultural and food industry in the UK (Felbermayr et al., 2017).

Estimates by experts from PricewaterhouseCoopers (2016) indicate that the potential countries with the largest GDP losses are Ireland, the Netherlands and Belgium. Trade between these countries and the UK is relatively large, which makes them particularly vulnerable to Brexit. In particular, the Irish economy is heavily dependent on trade with the UK: 14% of Ireland's exports and 34% of Ireland's imports depend on it. Apart from trade distortions, the reintroduction of a customs frontier would generate new costs and lead to a loss of time in trans-border transactions. On the other hand, Ireland could benefit from increased influxes of foreign investment and alternative locations, as foreign companies could look for other gateways to the EU single market. In turn, the Netherlands is the UK's second-largest trading partner in the EU, in terms of both volume and share of exports and imports. Moreover, the Netherlands maintains close investment links with the UK as the latter is the most popular destination for Dutch investors and the former is the second most popular destination for British investors. The increase in the euro's value against the British pound is an important factor that affects trade in the UK and the Netherlands.

In the weeks immediately after the Brexit vote, Dutch flower exporters reported a decrease in British demand for relatively expensive flowers and plants. Experts from the Netherlands Bureau for Economic Policy Analysis (Rojas-Romagosa, 2016) emphasize that the Netherlands has higher trade flows than the EU-27 average. Therefore, the country's losses in trade and GDP will also be higher. Their main scenarios assume that Dutch GDP will decrease by about 1.2% in the case of hard Brexit. On the other hand, should the UK and the EU reach a trade agreement, it will reduce losses to 0.9% level. Still, in such a scenario, they will remain significant. If we assume that potential trade would also generate changes in innovations, then the Dutch losses after Brexit would be much higher, since Dutch GDP would decline by 2%, as innovations positively affect productivity.

In PricewaterhouseCoopers (2016) ranking, Germany is the country that will probably be the least affected by Brexit. Brexit will eliminate many of the benefits of the single market for the German industry, especially in the automotive sector. German exports are likely to suffer more than imports, but since Germany is the EU's largest economy, it is relatively little dependent on trade with the UK.

Surveys conducted by the Association of German Chambers of Industry and Commerce (Deutscher Industrie- und Handelskammerntag, 2018) show that Brexit's influence on German companies will be predominantly negative in business, investment and commercial terms.[5] Companies expected a significant deterioration of the economic situation in 2018 (Figure 3.2). German companies that trade or invest in the UK consider the current state of their business to be satisfactory: 29% rate their business situation in the UK as good, but every fourth company considers its situation poor. For comparison, German companies rate the current business situation with other EU countries with a positive net result of 46%. Companies expect their UK business operations to significantly deteriorate over the next 12 months, although there are many more pessimists than optimists. The former group amounts to 36%, whereas the

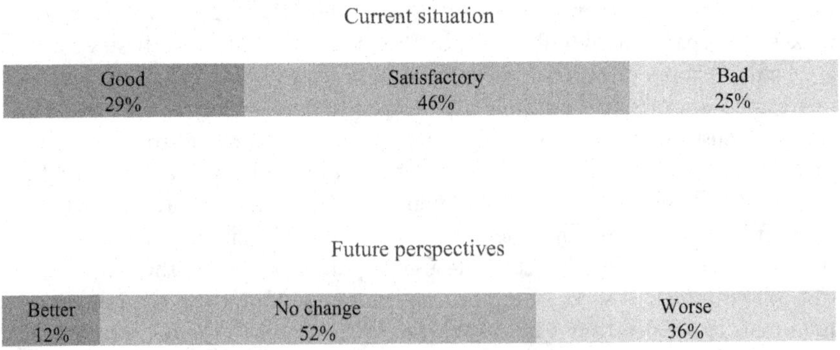

Current situation

Good 29%	Satisfactory 46%	Bad 25%

Future perspectives

Better 12%	No change 52%	Worse 36%

Figure 3.2 German entrepreneurs' attitudes toward Brexit (%)

Source: Own elaboration based on Deutsche Industrie- und Handelskammern (2018, p. 4).

latter – 12%. Companies that import from the UK are particularly pessimistic, as are the representatives of metal and automotive industries who are the least optimistic about their business prospects.

Currently, approximately 8% of German companies that invest in the UK plan to move their investments to other markets, although the exact conditions of Brexit are not yet known. Companies hope to ease the negative impact of the loss of membership in the internal market with a relocation of investments. While a change in production is costly in the short term, withdrawal from the UK provides additional certainty in the long-term perspective. It remains unclear how the British government will encourage investors to invest in the UK after Brexit. As the benefits of the internal market are unlikely to be available after Brexit, German companies plan to transfer their investments mainly to the internal market of the other EU-27 countries. About half of the companies consider moving their investments to Germany, another EU country, Switzerland or Norway, while one-third of them consider the future target region to lie outside Europe.

Moreover, the Association of German Chambers of Industry and Commerce (Deutsche Industrie- und Handelskammern, 2018) forecasts that the introduction of duties after Brexit will affect at least 30,000 German companies that export to the UK. Besides, approximately 40,000 companies will have to deal with non-standard declarations because they import goods from the UK. In the opinion of the Chamber, the associated costs and difficulties are as follows:[6]

- the number of additional customs declarations amounting to approximately 14.6 million per year;
- the cost of the total number of customs declarations amounting to approximately €200 million per year; and
- the cost of the total number of preferential proofs of origin amounting to approximately €300 million per year.

In this context, Brexit will be particularly harmful to two groups of companies as follows:

- Companies that have so far only traded in the single market. Therefore, they are unfamiliar with non-standard procedures. These are often small- or medium-sized enterprises (SMEs).
- Companies with internationalized and complex production chains that export and import multiple times to process goods before they complete their product. The process requires a customs declaration each time.

Furthermore, the UK's decision to leave the EU raises questions about the impact of Brexit on the Polish economy. Borowski, Olipra, and Błaszczyński (2018) indicate the possible effects of hard Brexit on Polish exporters. For years, the UK remained one of the primary recipients of Polish export goods, second only to Germany. According to the results of Borowski, Olipra and

Błaszczyński's model, the imposition of ad valorem duties by an average amount of 4.55% in the adopted "hard" Brexit scenario leads to, ceteris paribus, a decrease in the annual dynamics of Polish exports to the UK by approximately 1.3 percentage points in the first year after Brexit. Given that in 2016 Poland directed about 7% of its exports to the UK, the impact on the dynamics of all Polish exports would be equal to a decrease of 0.1 percentage points. On the other hand, relatively low labor costs in Poland and an attractive location in the center of Europe may encourage some British companies to relocate their operations to Poland. Such actions would let the British reduce production costs and maintain free access to the EU single market. In turn, it would have a positive impact on Polish exports, including exports to the UK.

Most studies listed in this chapter project losses in trade and income in both the UK and the EU, but the differences in the results presented in individual studies are significant (cf. Table 3.5 for a comparative analysis of projections for the UK). The experts explained most differences with the type of future arrangements (i.e., the scenario) between the UK and the EU and the channels of impact included in the estimates. In general, the impact of Brexit will depend on the speed, extent and direction of the effects of reducing the openness of the British economy.

Table 3.5 Comparative analysis of forecasts for the UK

Author	Channel	Forecast
Pricewaterhouse Coopers (2016)	Uncertainty, fiscal and trade channels, migration	−1.2% GDP in case of soft Brexit −3.5% GDP in case of hard Brexit (in year 2030)
Oxford Economics (2016)	Impact of choices regarding regulations, migration and fiscal policy on economic conditions	−0.1% GDP in case of soft Brexit −3.9% GDP in case of hard Brexit
Booth et al. (2015)	Fiscal and trade channels	−0.8% GDP in case of soft Brexit −2.2% GDP in case of hard Brexit
Ottaviano et al. (2014)	Fiscal and trade channels	−1.1% GDP in case of soft Brexit −3.1% GDP in case of hard Brexit
HM Treasury (2016)	Trade channels, FDI, productivity	−3.8% GDP in case of soft Brexit −7.5% GDP in case of hard Brexit
Breinlich, Leromain, Novy, and Sampson (2019)	Fiscal and trade channels	−1.6% GDP per capita in case of soft Brexit −3.3% GDP per capita in case of hard Brexit
Berthou et al. (2019)	Trade channels, migration	−2% GDP in case of soft Brexit −6% GDP in case of hard Brexit

Source: own elaboration.

Conclusions

The literature review clearly demonstrates that the UK's withdrawal from the EU will involve high economic and political costs, and that the outcome of the Brexit negotiations will shape relations between the EU and the UK for many years to come. The selected research results presented in this chapter include both positive and negative effects of Brexit for the UK. On the positive side, the British may experience tax savings that result from the partial removal of contributions to the EU and smaller economic distortions caused by potentially lower external barriers to trade. On the other hand, besides the main losses caused by limited trade integration, the UK may also expect future losses. These losses will result from the fact that the UK will not participate in new EU trade agreements and reductions in NTBs in the internal market.

The above analyses show that the British economy will grow in all scenarios, but this growth will be slower compared to a scenario in which the UK would have stayed in the EU. Many economists also expect the British pound to lose value in the event of a hard Brexit. If this were to happen, the price of imports would rise, which would cause a rise in inflation. The said rise in inflation is similar to the immediate post-Brexit referendum situation. In turn, a rise in inflation would result in a loss of purchasing power for businesses and consumers. Exports from the UK would become internationally cheaper, which would potentially mitigate some of the consequences of trade distortions with the EU. These figures are broadly consistent across most of the literature, both before and after the referendum.

We should remember that although the UK does leave the EU, there remains great potential for future cooperation. The interested parties may cooperate not only in trade relations but also in such areas as science, education, culture, and foreign and security policy. Avoiding negotiation failure and minimizing the cost of Brexit should now be the main task of politicians on both sides.

Notes

1 Parts of the Chapter 3 were based on the Authors' previous paper, i.e. Marian Gorynia, & Ewa Mińska-Struzik (2018). Globalizacja versus deglobalizacja – co jest lepsze dla świata i Polski? *Biuletyn PTE 3*(82), 40–50.
2 Researchers used the UK input-output tables to construct import exposure measures at the product level. They then combined these measures with the inflation experience in the UK before and after the Brexit referendum in June 2016, while controlling the impact of oil price developments and inflation in the euro area.
3 The applied model assumes perfectly competitive companies and does not include dynamic investment effects through capital accumulation, foreign direct investment, or any other growth-enhancing effects, e.g., through higher technical progress.
4 PricewaterhouseCoopers (2016) conducted a very comprehensive survey. The authors utilized the CGE model for the UK economy, particularly given the effects of changes in migration policy and higher uncertainty shortly after Brexit.
5 The experts conducted the "Going International 2018" study in February 2018 with the support of 79 Chambers of Industry and Commerce in Germany. Over 2,100 German

companies with foreign operations partook in the survey. Notably, 900 companies with large business contacts in the UK provided 43% of all responses.
6 These figures reflect cautious estimates as they are based on questionnaires filled by representatives of German companies who are familiar with filling customs declarations and preparing preferential proofs of origin.

References

Armstrong, A. (2016). *Comparing Brexit forecasts: Who should we believe on the economy?* Retrieved October 20, 2018 from http://ukandeu.ac.uk/comparing-brexit-forecasts-who-should-we-believe-on-the-economy/

Becker, S. O., Fetzer, T., & Novy, D. (2017). Who voted for Brexit? A comprehensive district-level analysis. *Economic Policy, 32*(92), 601–650. https://doi.org/10.1093/epolic/eix012

Berthou, A., Haincourt, S., de la Serve, M.-E., Estrada, A., Roth, M. A., & Kadow, A. (2019). Assessing the macroeconomic impact of Brexit through trade and migration channels. *Occasional Papers, 1911.* Retrieved from https://ideas.repec.org/p/bde/opaper/1911.html

Bevington, M., Huang, H., Menon, A., Portes, J., Rutter, J., & Sampson, T. (2019). *The economic impact of Boris Johnson's Brexit proposals.* CEP Brexit Analysis, 16. Retrieved from https://ukandeu.ac.uk/wp-content/uploads/2019/10/The-economic-impact-of-Boris-Johnsons-Brexit-proposals.pdf

Bhagwati, J. (2004). *In defence of globalization.* Oxford: Oxford University Press.

Booth, S., Howarth, Ch., Persson, M., Ruparel, R., & Swidli, P. (2015). *What if . . . ?The consequences, challenges & opportunities facing Britain outside EU.* OE Report. Retrieved from http://europas-krisen.zdf.de/media/downloads/Brexit/150507-Open-Europe-What-If-Report-Final-Digital-Copy.pdf

Borowski, J., Olipra, J., & Błaszyński, P. (2018). The impact of hard Brexit on Polish exports. *International Journal of Management and Economics, 54*(2), 99–109. https://doi.org/10.2478/ijme-2018-0010

Breinlich, H., Leromain, E., Novy, D., & Sampson, T. (2017). *The consequences of the Brexit vote for UK, inflation and living standards: First evidence.* Centre for Economic Performance (CEP) Brexit Analysis, 1. Retrieved from http://personal.lse.ac.uk/sampsont/VoteInflation_TP.pdf

Breinlich, H., Leromain, E., Novy, D., & Sampson, T. (2019). *Exchange rates and consumer prices: Evidence from Brexit.* Centre for Economic Performance (CEP) Brexit Analysis, 1. Retrieved from https://cep.lse.ac.uk/pubs/download/dp1667.pdf

Brown, J. (1992). Corporations as community: A new image for a new era. In J. Rensch (Ed.), *New traditions in business* (pp. 123–140). San Francisco, CA: Berrett-Koehler Publishers.

Colantone, I., & Stanig, P. (2018). Global competition and Brexit. *American Political Science Review, 112*(2), 201–218. https://doi.org/10.1017/S0003055417000685

Deutscher Industrie- und Handelskammertag. (2018). *The impact of Brexit on German businesses.* Retrieved from www.ihk-nuernberg.de/de/media/PDF/en/dihk-impact-of-brexit.pdf

Dhingra, S., Machin, S., & Overman, H. G. (2017). Local economic effects of Brexit. *National Institute Economic Review, 242*(1), 24–36. https://doi.org/10.1177/002795011724200112

Dhingra, S., & Sampson, T. (2019). Brexit economics. In *The research evidence on key issues for voters in the 2019 UK General election.* London: Centre for Economic Performance. Retrieved from https://cep.lse.ac.uk/pubs/download/ea048.pdf

Dicken, P. (1998). *Global shift*. New York: Guilford Press.

Dunning, J. H. (2003). *Making globalization good: The moral challenges of global capitalism*. Oxford: Oxford University Press.

Economist. (2017). *Deal or no deal? The siren song of a no-deal Brexit*. Retrieved November 2, 2017 from www.economist.com/britain/2017/11/30/the-siren-song-of-a-no-deal-brexit

European Movement International. (2017). *The consequences of a British exit from the European Union*. Retrieved from https://europeanmovement.eu/wp-content/uploads/2016/05/EMI_16_PolicyPosition_Brexit_17_VIEW_FINAL.pdf

Felbermayr, G., Fuest, C., Gröschl, J. K., & Stöhlker, D. (2017). *Economic effects of Brexit on the European economy*. EconPol Policy Report, 4. Retrieved from www.ifo.de/DocDL/EconPol_Policy_Report_04_2017_Brexit.pdf

Gilpin, R. (2000). *The challenge of global capitalism: The world economy in the 21st century*. Princeton, NJ: Princeton University Press.

Gomułka, S. (2016). Instytucje a mechanizmy długo i średniookresowego wzrostu gospodarczego w skali globalnej (Institutions and the mechanisms of long-term and medium-term economic growth on a global scale). *Studia Ekonomiczne, 90*(3), 343–352. Retrieved from http://inepan.pl/wp-content/uploads/2016/08/SE_2016_3_Gomulka.pdf

Gorynia, M. (2002). Internationalisation of economy versus economic policy under integration and globalization. *Poznań University of Economics Review, 2*(2), 5–19. Retrieved from www.ebr.edu.pl/volume2/issue2/2002_2_5.pdf

Gorynia, M. (2017a). Polska w obliczu procesów internacjonalizacji, globalizacji i integracji (Poland in the face of internationalization, globalization and integration processes). In J. Wilkin (Ed.), *Globalizacja, integracja europejska a suwerenność państwa (Globalization, European integration and national sovereignty)* (pp. 83–100). Warsaw: Komitet Prognoz "Polska 2000 Plus" przy Prezydium PAN.

Gorynia, M. (2017b). Nowy pragmatyzm. Jak jest z nim naprawdę? (New pragmatism: What is it really about?). *Rzeczpospolita*. Retrieved from www.rp.pl/Rzecz-o-polityce/302219914-Nowy-pragmatyzm-Jak-jest-z-nim-naprawde.html

Gorynia, M., & Kowalski, T. (2008). *Globalne i krajowe uwarunkowania funkcjonowania polskich przedsiębiorstw* (Global and domestic conditions affecting the operation of business in Poland). *Ekonomista, 1,* 51–76. Retrieved from www.researchgate.net/publication/255485840_Globalne_i_krajowe_uwarunkowania_funkcjonowania_polskich_przedsiebiorstw

Gorynia, M., & Mińska-Struzik, E. (2018). Globalizacja versus deglobalizacja – co jest lepsze dla świata i Polski? (Globalization versus deglobalization – What is better for the world and Poland?). *Biuletyn PTE, 3*(82), 50–60. Retrieved from www.researchgate.net/publication/327906247_Globalizacja_versus_deglobalizacja_-_co_jest_lepsze_dla_swiata_i_Polski_Biuletyn_Polskiego_Towarzystwa_Ekonomicznego_PTE

Götz, M. (2018). Przemysł czwartej generacji (przemysł 4.0) a międzynarodowa współpraca gospodarcza. *Ekonomista, 4,* 385–403. Retrieved from www.pte.pl/pliki/1/8905/Ekonomista2018-4-strony-8-26.pdf

HM Treasury. (2016). *HM Treasury analysis: The long-term economic impact of EU membership and the alternatives*. Retrieved from https://assets.publishing.service.gov.uk/government/uploads/system/uploads/attachment_data/file/517415/treasury_analysis_economic_impact_of_eu_membership_web.pdf

Kołodko, G. (2013). *Dokąd zmierza świat. Ekonomia polityczna przyszłości (Where is the world going: Political economy of the future)*. Warsaw: Prószyński i S-ka.

Kołodko, G. (2014). Nowy Pragmatyzm, czyli ekonomia i polityka dla przyszłości. *Ekonomista, 2,* 161–180. Retrieved from file:///C:/Users/USER/AppData/Local/Temp/PAN20ekonomista202014202201.pdf

Kołodko, G., & Koźmiński, A. (2017). *Nowy pragmatyzm kontra nowy nacjonalizm (New pragmatism versus new nationalism)*. Warsaw: Prószyński i S-ka.

Kowalski, T. (2013). *Globalisation and transformation in central European countries: The case of Poland*. Poznań: Poznań University of Economics Press.

Manyika, J., Lund, S., Bughin, J., Woetzel, J., Stamenov, K., & Dhingra, D. (2016). *Digital globalization: The new era of global flows*. McKinsey Global Institute. Retrieved from www.mckinsey.com/business-functions/mckinsey-digital/our-insights/digital-globalization-the-new-era-of-global-flows#s

McCann, L. (2018). *A very short, fairly interesting and reasonably cheap book about globalization*. Los Angeles, CA: Sage.

Michie, J. (2017). *Advanced introduction to globalisation*. Cheltenham: Edward Elgar.

Milward, B. (2003). *Globalisation? Internationalisation and monopoly capitalism. Historical processes and capitalist dynamism*. Cheltenham: Edward Elgar.

Nederveen, P. J. (2012). Periodizing globalization: Histories of globalization. *New Global Studies, 6*(2), 1–25. https://doi.org/10.1515/1940-0004.1174

Ohmae, K. (1995). *The end of the nation state*. New York: Free Press.

Orłowski, W. (2016). Czy globalizacja, którą znamy, przetrwa? (Will the globalization we know survive?). In M. Bałkowski (Ed.), *Ekonomia przyszłości. Wokół nowego pragmatyzmu Grzegorza W. Kołodko (Economics of the future: Towards the new pragmatism of Grzegorz W. Kołodko)*. Warszaw: Wydawnictwo Naukowe PWN.

Ottaviano, G., Pessoa, J. P., Sampson, T., & Reenen, J. (2014). *The costs and benefits of leaving the EU*. CFS Working Paper, 472. Retrieved from https://papers.ssrn.com/sol3/papers.cfm?abstract_id=2506664

Oxford Economics. (2016). *Assessing the economic implications of Brexit*. Retrieved from: https://www.oxfordeconomics.com/recent-releases/assessing-the-economic-implications-of-brexit

Parker, B. B. (1998). *Globalization and business practice: Managing across boundaries*. London: Sage Publications.

PricewaterhouseCoopers. (2016). *Leaving the EU: Implications for the UK economy*. Retrieved from www.pwc.co.uk/economic-services/assets/leaving-the-eu-implications-for-the-uk-economy.pdf

Primo Braga, C. A. (2017). The threat of economic disintegration. In C. A. Primo Braga & B. Hoekman (Eds.), *Future of global trade order* (2nd ed.). San Domenico di Fiesole: EUI, IMD & FDC. https://doi.org/10.2870/169287

Rodrik, D. (2011). *The globalization paradox: Why global markets, states and democracy can't coexists*. Oxford: Oxford University Press.

Rodrik, D. (2018). Populism and the economics of globalization. *Journal of International Business Policy, 1*, 12–33. https://doi.org/10.1057/s42214-018-0001-4

Rojas-Romagosa, H. (2016). *Trade effects of Brexit for the Netherlands*. CPB Netherlands Bureau for Economic Policy. Retrieved from www.cpb.nl/sites/default/files/omnidownload/CPB-Backgroud-Document-June-2016-Trade-effects-of-brexit-for-the-netherlands.pdf

Stiglitz, J. E. (2002). *Globalization and its discontents*. Washington, DC: W.W. Norton Company.

Stiglitz, J. E. (2004). *Globalizacja (Globalization)*. Warsaw: PWN.

Stiglitz, J. E. (2008). The future of global governance. In N. Serra & J. E. Stiglitz (Eds.), *The Washington consensus reconsidered: Towards a new global governance*. Oxford: Oxford University Press.

Stiglitz, J. E. (2011). The failure of macroeconomics in America. *China & World Economy, 19*(5), 17–30. https://doi.org/10.1111/j.1749-124X.2011.01256.x

Streeten, P. (1998). Globalisation. Threat or opportunity? *The Pakistan Development Review*, 37(4), 51–83.

Szymański, W. (2007). *Czy globalizacja musi być irracjonalna? (Does globalization have to be irrational?)*. Warsaw: Oficyna Wydawnicza SGH.

Yip, G. S. (1995). *Total global strategy: Managing for worldwide competitive advantage*. Englewood Cliffs, NJ & London: Prentice Hall.

Yip, G. S. (2001). *Total global strategy*. Englewood Cliffs, NJ & London: Prentice Hall.

Ziewiec, G. (2012). *Trzy fale globalizacji. Rozwój, nadzieje i rozczarowania (Three waves of globalization: Growth, hopes and disappointments)*. Warsaw: Instytut Nauk Ekonomicznych Polskiej Akademii Nauk.

4 Where do we stand? EU–27 vulnerability in the face of the Brexit uncertainty

Comparative analysis

Anna Matysek-Jędrych,
Katarzyna Mroczek-Dąbrowska

Introduction

Although equality has been and still is one of the EU's most prized features, Brexit will undoubtedly impact each member state. Although all countries trade, invest and move around the UK, not all countries fear the UK's withdrawal in the same way. The sources of their uncertainty are manifold: the fear of trade tariff and nontariff restrictions, restrictions on cash flow, the EU budget shortfall, movement limitations, work permits and political relations. Depending on the shape of the final agreement between the EU and the UK, Brexit impact is bound to differ. However, we may still attempt to assess the EU-27 vulnerability toward Brexit based on economic assumptions such as trade, investment and migration. Such a perspective ensures relatively unbiased ground for estimating how countries should endeavor to negotiate the post-Brexit perspective.

Vulnerability: the concept and measure

The word "vulnerability" comes from the Latin *vulnerare* and seems to be an abstract concept, difficult to measure and difficult to define. There are a few reasons that we face terminological and semantic chaos in this matter. First, although the word "vulnerability" is widely used – sometimes even without thorough consideration – there remains no universally agreed definition. Second, vulnerability is a multidimensional notion that covers different issues and is dynamic by nature, hence impossible to reduce to a single equation (Birkmann, 2006; Downing, 2004; Schneiderbauer & Ehrlich, 2006). Third, the ability to properly assess and measure vulnerability appears crucial from a functional perspective. This ability could aid us in estimating the potential consequences of both rapid and crawling events.

The literature encompasses numerous attempts to systematize the concept of vulnerability (Bohle, 2001; Downing et al., 2006; Green, 2004; Luers, 2005; Turner et al., 2003; Wisner, Blaikie, Cannon, & Davis, 2004). Although, vulnerability is perceived through the lens of its multifaceted nature and we cannot

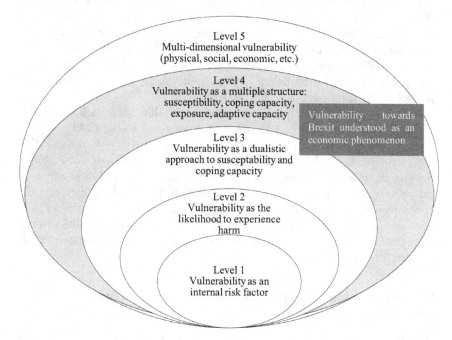

Figure 4.1 The key spheres of vulnerability

Source: Own elaboration based on Birkmann (2006).

precisely define it, we may agree that vulnerability is a scientific concept (Bogardi & Birkmann, 2004). One of its well-known definitions was formulated by Cardona (2004), who views vulnerability as a system of an entity's physical, economic, social or political susceptibility to destruction in the result of a risky event. Exposition to risk is the core feature of vulnerability (the inner circle in Figure 4.1). Thus, the definition of vulnerability can be extended to cover other dimensions and spheres, beyond the human-centered approach (see Figure 4.1).

Other authors, e.g., Vogel and O'Brien (2004) stress the features of vulnerability, instead of defining the term as such. They describe vulnerability as *multi-dimensional, differential, scale-dependent and dynamic*. It means that vulnerability is to vary across entities in relation to time, space and units, and changes over time.

Different approaches to defining vulnerability effect in various conceptual frameworks, which create the next step toward the development of a vulnerability measure. Bohle (2001) believes the vulnerability's structure has two sides: an external one and an internal one. The internal side relates to the capacity to anticipate, cope with and resist risk while the external one covers exposure to risk. Bohle's double structure of vulnerability offers a good starting point for creating a complex framework. Another – conceptual – framework is a proposal by the disaster risk community, which distinguishes four categories (Bollin, Cardenas, Hahn, & Vatsa, 2003; Davidson, 1997): hazard, exposure, vulnerability and capacity. In contrast to the double-sided structure by Bohle (2001), the disaster risk school perceives vulnerability as a component of risk. Turner et al. (2003) define vulnerability more broadly as their analytical framework covers three separate elements: exposure, sensitivity and resilience. The important difference between Turner et al.'s (2003) proposal and the two frameworks above relates to the linked human-environment context, which forms the essence of Turner et al.'s analytical framework.

The most advanced analytical framework – a holistic approach to vulnerability – stems from two models: one by Cardona and Barbat (2000) and the other one by Bogardi and Birkmann (2004) and Cardona (1999), the so-called BBC framework. Both models consider several dimensions of vulnerability, dividing them into three main categories (factors) of vulnerability: exposure and physical susceptibility, social and economic fragility, and the luck of resilience or ability to cope and recover. The BBC framework appears as even more advanced mostly because of its broad applicability and direct links to the concept of sustainable development (for more, see Bogardi & Birkmann, 2004; Cardona, 1999).

The construction of a synthetic indicator for economic vulnerability to Brexit

As mentioned earlier, the word "vulnerability" originated from the Latin *vulnerare*, which in direct translation means "to wound" (Briguglio, 2016, p. 1058). Therefore, a vulnerability index must reflect both exposure to an occurrence and risks that this occurrence entails. In country-specific terms, economic vulnerability commonly appears as "country's susceptibility to being harmed by external economic forces as a result of exposure to such forces" (Briguglio, 2016, p. 1058). In our case, this external force would be the threat of UK leaving the EU structures.

The vulnerability analysis often draws on sustainability science in which the framework was built and since adapted in other research areas, including economics (Briguglio, Cordina, Farrugia, & Vella, 2009). The vulnerability analysis seeks answers to the following questions. Who and why is the subject of various socioeconomic changes? What are the consequences of these changes and what can amplify them? What can be done to reduce uncertainty and vulnerability to changes? Who and why is more resilient to incessant changes (Turner et al., 2003, p. 8074)? Therefore, the concept suggests that vulnerability can be viewed as a three-dimensional phenomenon that encompasses the following (Figure 4.2):

*   exposure to an occurrence;
*   sensitivity to an occurrence; and
*   resilience to an occurrence.

The exposure component is seen as inherent and permanent, i.e., it does not stem directly from policies or governance[1] and is not easily changed in time.

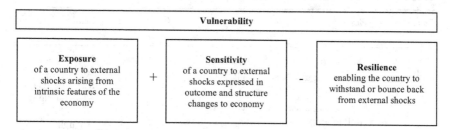

Figure 4.2 The vulnerability context as a three-dimensional phenomenon

Source: Own elaboration based on Briguglio (2016) and Turner et al. (2003).

It reflects on the country's proneness to exogenous shocks. The sensitivity component determines in what way the country is affected by the exogenous shock. This can concern both the performance of the country and the changes caused to the structure of the economy. Ultimately, the resilience component expresses whether a country is able to quickly absorb or bounce back from the adverse occurrence. The exposure and sensitivity add to an increased vulnerability of a country while higher resilience decreases it (Figure 4.2). Here, the economic vulnerability to Brexit will also be determined with the use of the three aforementioned lenses: exposure, sensitivity and resilience (Table 4.1).

The indicators suggested in the exposure perspective refer directly to a country's openness.[2] However, we express them here as individual measures and additionally broke them down into two main categories: production and service industries. These are mostly perceived as an inherent feature (Briguglio et al., 2009) since they are conditioned by the size of the country's home market and demand, but also the availability of resources and country's ability to efficiently produce the goods and services required to satisfy home country demand.

Therefore, a country with high economic openness to foreign trade is relatively more exposed to external occurrences over which it holds little or no control. On the other hand, export and import concentration – which refer to the structure of the country's foreign trade operations – refer not to the extent (intensity) of the UK-EU relations but to the sectoral structure of bilateral relations. The literature review reveals that high concentration exacerbates sensitivity toward a certain shock because it prevents an economy from creating losses in one area with gains in other areas. Nevertheless, with an increase in product concentration we may also expect improved competitiveness; thus, the results can be ambiguous. Here, we focus on two groups of products: agricultural and high-tech ones. Agricultural products are sensitive to trade restrictions and are predominantly exported by countries seen as less competitive in comparison to high-tech products, which are less prone to suffer from trade changes, and they dominate in more competitive economies (Nazarczuk et al., 2018). We analyze concentration levels from both the market penetration (exports) and resource-seeking perspective (imports). Moreover, we enhance the analysis with a relatively rarely undertaken issue of migration. Migration does not only have

Table 4.1 Vulnerability to Brexit – variable operationalization

Dimension of vulnerability	Variables	Impact on Brexit vulnerability	Similar usage
Exposure	Exports sent to UK as % of GDP (goods)	+	Nazarczuk, Umiński, and Márquez-Ramos (2018); Briguglio et al. (2009), Briguglio (2016)
	Exports sent to UK as % of GDP (services)	+	
		+	
	Imports sent to each country as % of GDP (goods)	+	
	Imports sent to each country as % of GDP (services)		
Sensitivity	**Export product concentration:**	+	Nazarczuk et al. (2018), Herzer and Nowak-Lehnmann (2006)
	– Share of agricultural products exported to UK	–	
	– Share of high-tech products exported to UK	+	
	Import product concentration:	–	
		+	
	– Share of agricultural products imported from UK	+	
	– Share of high-tech products imported from UK		
	Migration:		
	– Share of immigrants from UK to country's population		
	– Share of immigrants to UK to country's population		
Adaptive capacity	Quality of institutions – EU Regional Quality of Government index	–	Nazarczuk et al. (2018), Briguglio et al. (2009), Briguglio (2016)
		–	
	FDI stock from UK as % of GDP	–	
	FDI stock in UK as % of GDP	–	
	Innovative capacity – EU Regional Innovation Scoreboard	–	
	Quality of human capital – proxied by the share of population aged 24–65 with tertiary education	–	

Source: Own elaboration.

a social aspect – manifest in the issue of free movement – but it also reveals a significant economic element. Migrants accounted for nearly 70% increase in workforce in Europe between 2004 and 2014, thus significantly altering the labor market flexibility and capacity among the EU member states (OECD, 2014). Since the inflow of migrants was mentioned as one of the reasons for Brexit, we include it in our analysis while stressing that migration does have an economic angle. However, we only analyze net migration among individual countries, i.e., we only consider the movement of people who originate from the EU-28 states. Another aspect that we wished to consider in the sensitivity area were the *FDI flows*, including both the FDI inflow into the UK and the FDI outflow to individual EU member states. This would enable us to include the equity-focused relations between the countries. However, the initial data analysis indicated that – due to statistical reasons – this variable had to be excluded from the dataset.

The adaptive capabilities or, in other words, the economy's resilience expresses to what degree can a country overcome the uncertainty arising from Brexit. Here, we include various dimensions of economy's functioning. We focus on the institutional quality that should provide foundations for stabilizing economies in the face of external shocks and facilitate a quicker comeback to the pre-shock state. Likewise, we include the aspect of innovativeness which – according to the World Global Forum (Schwab, 2016) – now prompts economies to fast-track from efficiency-driven economies to innovation-driven and most developed ones. Therefore, we assume that the more innovative an economy, the higher the probability it overcomes the negative outcomes of Brexit. Similarly, the more highly educated and specialized workforce the economy has, the more insensitive will it remain to the net migration effect. Finally, we focus on long-term investment relations between the UK and the remaining EU members understood as *FDI stocks*. Many assume that European companies with established equity presence in the UK, and vice versa, will be interested in mitigating Brexit's adverse consequences (Nazarczuk et al., 2018) with the networking effect. As a point of reference, we selected 2013–2015 since these years represent the post-2008 crisis period and refer to the timeline yet not "tainted" with the post-Brexit referendum.

Following Nazarczuk et al. (2018),[3] we aimed to establish which of the EU-27 member states were most prone to suffer from the UK withdrawal from the Common Market. The indicators listed in Table 4.1 were taken into analysis and included in the final *vulnerability measure*. The variables were normalized to make them mutually comparable. We have applied the unitarization method, separately for stimulants and destimulants. The synthetic indicator did not include weighting since "the theoretical knowledge does not allow for the hypotheses to be consistently derived on differential weightings" (Maggino & Ruviglioni, 2009, p. 3). In such a case, we do not prejudge that some of the variables hold more influence over other. The results in the exposure, sensitivity and resilience dimensions – along with the overall vulnerability measure – were clustered into four groups (Nazarczuk et al., 2018, p. 8):

group 1: $dim_i \geq \overline{\overline{dim}} + SDdim$;
group 2: $\overline{\overline{dim}} \leq dim_i < \overline{\overline{dim}} + SDdim$;
group 3: $\overline{\overline{dim}} - SDdim \leq dim_i < \overline{\overline{dim}}$;
group 4: $dim_i < \overline{\overline{dim}} - SDdim$,

in which $\overline{\overline{dim}}$ stands for mean value of a specific dimension and *SDdim* stands for standard deviation of the indicator.

The variables were revised for sufficient spatial variability where in each case the coefficient of variation exceeded the threshold value of 0.2. Furthermore, we applied correlation analysis which indicated that each item exceeded the value of 0.55. Therefore, considering commonly accepted standards (Nunnally, 1978), we may conclude that all the items can be included in the creation of the vulnerability degree. Cronbach's alpha reliability test reported a score of around 0.78 for exposure, 0.76 for sensitivity and 0.84 for resilience. The overall vulnerability measure indicated Cronbach's alpha at the level of 0.88. The threshold value for accepting the measure as reliable is 0.7. However, some studies claim that even scores above the value of 0.6 can be ruled as adequate (cf. Szymura-Tyc, 2013). Factor analysis proved that all sub-factors are worth keeping.

EU-27 member states' vulnerability to Brexit

The proposed exposure measure is supposed to illustrate the extent to which economies are prone to suffer trade-wise from the UK's withdrawal from the EU. The higher the value of the synthetic indicator, the greater the exposure to the Brexit consequences.

As our results indicate, the EU-27 economies display extreme, high or moderate exposure to Brexit consequences (Table 4.2 and Figure 4.3). None of

Table 4.2 Ranking of EU-27 member states' exposure to Brexit

Rank	Country	Exposure (0–1)	Group
1	Malta	0.70	Extremely exposed
2	Ireland	0.70	Extremely exposed
3	Cyprus	0.45	Extremely exposed
4	The Netherlands	0.40	Extremely exposed
5	Belgium	0.39	Extremely exposed
6	Luxembourg	0.37	Highly exposed
7	Czech Republic	0.20	Moderately exposed
8	Hungary	0.17	Moderately exposed
9	Lithuania	0.15	Moderately exposed
10	Slovakia	0.15	Moderately exposed
11	Sweden	0.15	Moderately exposed
12	Portugal	0.15	Moderately exposed
13	Germany	0.14	Moderately exposed
14	Latvia	0.13	Moderately exposed
15	Poland	0.13	Moderately exposed
16	Spain	0.13	Moderately exposed
17	Denmark	0.13	Moderately exposed
18	Bulgaria	0.11	Moderately exposed
19	France	0.11	Moderately exposed

Rank	Country	Exposure (0–1)	Group
20	Greece	0.09	Moderately exposed
21	Estonia	0.08	Moderately exposed
22	Finland	0.08	Moderately exposed
23	Italy	0.07	Moderately exposed
24	Romania	0.06	Moderately exposed
25	Austria	0.05	Moderately exposed
26	Slovenia	0.05	Moderately exposed
27	Croatia	0.05	Moderately exposed

Source: Own elaboration.

■ Extremely exposed   ■ Highly exposed   ■ Moderately exposed

Figure 4.3 Ranking of EU-27 member states' exposure to Brexit

Source: Own elaboration.

the countries was classified as unexposed (exposure score below 0.02). Malta, Ireland, Cyprus, the Netherlands and Belgium are the countries that most likely to suffer from the UK's withdrawal from the EU. These are either countries of geographical proximity to the UK (Ireland) or small economy that historically engendered strong ties to the UK (e.g., Cyprus and Malta). Just one country, Luxembourg, was listed as highly exposed whereas all the remaining 21 member states were classified as moderately exposed. The differences in exposure scores among these countries were relatively small.

Poland was listed in the middle of the exposure ranking (15th position) among the "moderate exposure" group. The most worrying factor was Poland's share of exports of goods to the UK to the generated GDP level. Poland exports consist of motor vehicles and spare parts, furniture, television receivers and automatic data processing machines. It is much less service-oriented, and services do not constitute the main trading area between the two countries. Similarly, Belgium, Ireland and the Netherlands are also most exposed in the exports of goods, whereas Cyprus, Malta and Luxembourg may worry more about services. On the imports side, Ireland and Malta might be forced to seek alternative suppliers of different goods, whereas only Malta is seriously exposed to suffer from the potential trade restrictions in services.

Table 4.3 and Figure 4.4 present the sensitivity scores for the EU-27 member states. The indicator is interpreted similarly as the exposure measure, which means that the higher the value of the score, the greater the sensitivity to the UK's withdrawal from the EU.

Table 4.3 Ranking of EU-27 member states' sensitivity to Brexit

Rank	Country	Sensitivity (0–1)	Group
1	Ireland	0.68	Extremely sensitive
2	The Netherlands	0.43	Extremely sensitive
3	Germany	0.43	Extremely sensitive
4	Cyprus	0.29	Highly sensitive
5	Belgium	0.28	Highly sensitive
6	France	0.23	Highly sensitive
7	Malta	0.23	Highly sensitive
8	Italy	0.21	Highly sensitive
9	Latvia	0.20	Highly sensitive
10	Czech Republic	0.18	Moderately sensitive
11	Lithuania	0.18	Moderately sensitive
12	Hungary	0.18	Moderately sensitive
13	Poland	0.17	Moderately sensitive
14	Slovakia	0.17	Moderately sensitive
15	Estonia	0.12	Moderately sensitive
16	Spain	0.12	Moderately sensitive
17	Slovenia	0.12	Moderately sensitive
18	Sweden	0.11	Moderately sensitive
19	Bulgaria	0.09	Moderately sensitive
20	Denmark	0.08	Moderately sensitive
21	Luxembourg	0.07	Moderately sensitive
22	Austria	0.07	Moderately sensitive
23	Portugal	0.07	Moderately sensitive
24	Romania	0.06	Moderately sensitive
25	Finland	0.05	Moderately sensitive
26	Croatia	0.03	Insensitive
27	Greece	0.01	Insensitive

Source: Own elaboration.

Figure 4.4 Ranking of EU-27 member states' sensitivity to Brexit

Source: Own elaboration.

This time, the results were more varied and classified the economies among the four groups: extremely, highly, moderately and unaffected. Once again, Ireland and the Netherlands turned out to be most sensitive to Brexit. Germany followed closely with a score similar to the one of the Netherlands. Germany exhibits particular sensitivity in the trade of high-tech products and services, which in its case is the most worrying factor of all EU-27 member states. Cyprus, Malta and Belgium are classified here as highly sensitive ones which could have been expected considering the exposure results. However, Luxembourg ranks very low, in the 21st position. This is due to the relatively positive net migration effect and high-tech trade. Once again, Poland places in the middle of the ranking (13th position) with none of the analyzed sub-indicators posing particular problems.

When analyzing the exposure and sensitivity rankings, we must remember that they do not necessarily suggest the same results, as in case of the Luxembourg. Exposure corresponds to the intensity of vulnerability while sensitivity analysis provides information on whether countries are or are not expected to suffer in the most important areas of socioeconomic relations; in this case, free trade and the free movement of people. However, in most of the cases, outcomes of the exposure and sensitivity analyses correlate, which only reinforces our conclusions.

The final analysis refers to the resilience capabilities of EU-27 member states (Table 4.4 and Figure 4.5). Again, the higher the achieved score, the more probable is the country to quickly cope with the difficulties posed by Brexit.

60   *Anna Matysek-Jędrych, Katarzyna Mroczek-Dąbrowska*

Table 4.4 Ranking of EU-27 member states' resilience to Brexit

Rank	Country	Resilience (0–1)	Group
1	The Netherlands	0.90	Extremely resilient
2	Germany	0.69	Extremely resilient
3	Denmark	0.67	Extremely resilient
4	Luxembourg	0.63	Extremely resilient
5	Ireland	0.63	Extremely resilient
6	Sweden	0.61	Extremely resilient
7	Finland	0.58	Highly resilient
8	Belgium	0.49	Highly resilient
9	Spain	0.47	Highly resilient
10	France	0.43	Highly resilient
11	Austria	0.43	Highly resilient
12	Cyprus	0.41	Highly resilient
13	Estonia	0.37	Moderately resilient
14	Lithuania	0.33	Moderately resilient
15	Slovenia	0.33	Moderately resilient
16	Portugal	0.27	Moderately resilient
17	Czech Republic	0.26	Moderately resilient
18	Malta	0.25	Moderately resilient
19	Latvia	0.25	Moderately resilient
20	Poland	0.22	Moderately resilient
21	Italy	0.21	Moderately resilient
22	Hungary	0.21	Moderately resilient
23	Greece	0.17	Moderately resilient
24	Slovakia	0.17	Not resilient
25	Croatia	0.13	Not resilient
26	Bulgaria	0.12	Not resilient
27	Romania	0.04	Not resilient

Source: Own elaboration.

The breakdown of the resilience analysis is more varied than the previous ones. The countries known as the most competitive ones (Northwestern Europe) are generally expected to tackle the post-Brexit issues with relative speed. Surprisingly, the UK's neighboring Ireland – an economy that ranked first in both the exposure and sensitivity analyses – is also expected to quickly return to pre-Brexit conditions. This is due to relatively stable institutions, highly assessed human capital and innovative capacity. Poland ranked 20th in the analysis, meaning that it is not expected to cope with the difficulties as well as other countries. Poland struggles in all those aspects that Ireland is doing well and – in comparison to other economies – Poland lacks sufficient networking capabilities. However, it is still in a better position than Slovakia, Croatia, Bulgaria and Romania, which are not resilient at all.

■ Extremely resilient ■ Highly resilient ■ Moderately resilient ■ Not resilient

Obsługiwane przez usługę Bing
© GeoNames, HERE, MSFT, Microsoft, Wikipedia

Figure 4.5 Ranking of EU-27 member states' resilience to Brexit
Source: Own elaboration.

Overall, when we combine the three perspectives – the threatening exposure and sensitivity to the UK's withdrawal from the EU and the adaptive capabilities that moderate these threats – we may conclude that there are four groups of vulnerability of EU-27 countries to Brexit (Table 4.5 and Figure 4.6).

Combining all three perspectives allows us to more fully comprehend the degree to which individual economies are expected to suffer Brexit's consequences. As expected, Ireland, Malta and Cyprus are the most vulnerable to the UK's withdrawal from the EU. However, the later positions in the ranking draw more attention. Countries that ranked quite moderately in exposure and sensitivity (e.g., Latvia and Poland) due to low adaptive capabilities are overall quite vulnerable to Brexit. Although the difference in score between the fourth and 14th rank is very low (0.05), economy-wise these countries can expect significant struggle. For instance, in Poland ca. 40,000 companies are estimated to uphold close trade ties with the British market. This means that hard Brexit could – in the case of lacking adaptive strategies – result in a drop of their trade performance. On the other end, we have the Scandinavian economies and Austria which – due to high competitiveness and diversity in internationalization – are not prone to suffer much from the consequences of Brexit.

Conclusions

The above analysis provides two important contributions. First, it indicates the vulnerability of the EU-27 member states toward UK's withdrawal from the Common Market: we may expect hardly any discernible impacts on economy

Table 4.5 Ranking of EU-27 member states' vulnerability to Brexit

Rank	Country	Vulnerability	Group
1	Ireland	0.61	Extremely vulnerable
2	Malta	0.52	Extremely vulnerable
3	Cyprus	0.44	Extremely vulnerable
4	Italy	0.37	Highly vulnerable
5	Latvia	0.35	Highly vulnerable
6	Poland	0.35	Highly vulnerable
7	Romania	0.35	Highly vulnerable
8	Belgium	0.34	Highly vulnerable
9	Hungary	0.33	Highly vulnerable
10	Bulgaria	0.33	Highly vulnerable
11	Slovakia	0.33	Highly vulnerable
12	Germany	0.33	Highly vulnerable
13	France	0.32	Highly vulnerable
14	Czech Republic	0.32	Highly vulnerable
15	Greece	0.31	Moderately vulnerable
16	Portugal	0.30	Moderately vulnerable
17	Lithuania	0.30	Moderately vulnerable
18	Croatia	0.30	Moderately vulnerable
19	The Netherlands	0.29	Moderately vulnerable
20	Spain	0.26	Moderately vulnerable
21	Estonia	0.25	Moderately vulnerable
22	Luxembourg	0.25	Moderately vulnerable
23	Slovenia	0.24	Moderately vulnerable
24	Austria	0.22	Not vulnerable
25	Sweden	0.21	Not vulnerable
26	Finland	0.18	Not vulnerable
27	Denmark	0.17	Not vulnerable

Source: Own elaboration.

in many EU countries. Second, the analysis offers emotionless fundamental information and adds an economic perspective to the undoubtedly difficult negotiation process that still lies ahead. Since none of the member states has invoked the Article 50 before, Brexit causes unexpected and unmeasurable volatility to all parties involved. Our study was driven by the strong belief that neither the UK nor the EU are interested in escalating tensions following Brexit and a European disintegration process. All stakeholders in the Brexit negotiation process have a stake in both the political and economic stability of Europe, which requires all countries to cooperate to create an optimum public policy response.

Extremely vulnerable   Highly vulnerable   Moderately vulnerable   Not vulnerable

Figure 4.6 Ranking of EU-27 member states' vulnerability to Brexit

Source: Own elaboration.

Notes

1 We may claim that exports and imports result from adaptive policies. However, it is structure (what is traded) rather than volume that are nurtured and not inherent.
2 The openness degree is generally expressed as (exports value + imports value)/GDP.
3 Nazarczuk, Umiński, and Márquez-Ramos (2018) conducted their study in a regional perspective, verifying which of the regions in Poland and Spain were the most vulnerable to negative Brexit trade effects.

References

Birkmann, J. (2006). Measuring vulnerability to promote disaster-resilient societies and to enhance adaptation: Conceptual frameworks and definitions. In J. Birkmann (Ed.), *Measuring vulnerability to natural hazards: Towards disaster resilient societies* (pp. 9–79). Tokyo: United Nations University Press.

Bogardi, J., & Birkmann, J. (2004). Vulnerability assessment: The first step towards sustainable risk reduction. In D. Malzahn & T. Plapp (Eds.), *Disaster and society – From hazard assessment to risk reduction*. Berlin: Logos Verlag.

Bohle, H. G. (2001). *Vulnerability and criticality: Perspectives from social geography*. IHDP Update 2/2001. International Human Dimensions Programme on the Global Environmental Change.

Bollin, C., Cardenas, C., Hahn, H., & Vatsa, K. S. (2003). *Natural disaster network: Disaster risk management by communities and local governments*. Washington, DC: Inter-American Development Bank.

Briguglio, L. (2016). Exposure to external shocks and economic resilience of countries: Evidence from global indicators. *Journal of Economic Studies*, *43*(6), 1057–1078. https://doi.org/10.1108/JES-12-2014-0203

Briguglio, L., Cordina, G., Farrugia, N., & Vella, S. (2009). Economic vulnerability and resilience: Concepts and measurements. *Oxford Development Studies, 37*(3), 229–247. https://doi.org/10.1080/13600810903089893

Cardona, O. D. (1999). Environmental management and disaster prevention: Two related topics: A holistic risk assessment and management approach. In J. Ingleton (Ed.), *Natural disaster management.* London: Tudor Rose.

Cardona, O. D. (2004). The need for rethinking the concepts of vulnerability and risk from a holistic perspective: A necessary review and criticism for effective risk management. In G. Bankoff, G. Frerks, & D. Hilhors (Eds.), *Mapping vulnerability: Disasters, development and people.* London: Earthscan Publishers.

Cardona, O. D., & Barbat, A. H. (2000). *El Riesgo Sísmico y su Prevención (Seismic risk and its prevention).* Cuaderno Técnico 5. Madrid: Calidad Siderúrgica.

Davidson, R. (1997). *An urban earthquake disaster risk index.* Department of Civil Engineering, Report No. 121. Stanford: Stanford University Press.

Downing, T. E. (2004). *What have we learned regarding a vulnerability science?* Buenos Aires: United Nations Framework Convention on Climate Change.

Downing, T. E., Aerts, J., Soussan, J., Barthelemy, O., Bharwani, S., Ionescu, C., . . . & Ziervogel, G. (2006). *Integrating social vulnerability into water management.* NeWater Working Paper No. 5. Retrieved from www.pik-potsdam.de/en/output/projects/projects-archive/favaia/pubs/downing_etal_2005.pdf

Green, C. (2004). The evaluation of vulnerability to flooding. *Disaster Prevention and Management, 13*(4), 323–329. https://doi.org/10.1108/09653560410556546

Herzer, D., & Nowak-Lehnmann, D. F. (2006). What does export diversification do for growth? An econometric analysis. *Applied Economics, 38*(15), 1825–1838. https://doi.org/10.1080/00036840500426983

Luers, A. L. (2005). The surface of vulnerability: An analytical framework for examining environmental change. *Global Environmental Change, 15*(3), 214–223. https://doi.org/10.1016/j.gloenvcha.2005.04.003

Maggino, F., & Ruviglioni, E. (2009). *Obtaining weights: From objective to subjective approaches in view of more participative methods in the construction of composite indicators. New techniques and technologies for statistics.* Brussels: European Commission. Retrieved from https://ec.europa.eu/eurostat/documents/1001617/4398464/POSTER-1A-OBTAINING-WEIGHTS-MAGGINO-RUVIGLIONI.pdf

Nazarczuk, J., Umiński, S., & Márquez-Ramos, L. (2018). *Vulnerability to the consequences of Brexit: Evidence for regions in Spain and Poland.* Conference paper.

Nunnally, J. C. (1978). *Psychomtietric theory.* New York: McGraw-Hill.

OECD. (2014). *Is migration good for the economy?* Retrieved from www.oecd.org/migration/OECD%20Migration%20Policy%20Debates%20Numero%202.pdf

Schneiderbauer, S., & Ehrlich, D. (2006). *Risk, hazard and people's vulnerability to natural hazards: A review of definitions, concepts and data.* Brussels: European Commission – Joint Research Centre. Retrieved from https://op.europa.eu/pl/publication-detail/-/publication/8b225579-50bc-4192-8343-e0459f8afccb

Schwab, K. (2016). *The global competitiveness report 2016–2017.* Geneva: World Economic Forum.

Szymura-Tyc, M. (2013). Measuring the degree of firms' internationalization at their early stages of international commitment. *Journal of Economics and Management, 13*(3), 101–118. Retrieved from file:///C:/Users/USER/AppData/Local/Temp/7_Szymura-Tyc_Measuring_the_degree_of_firms.pdf

Turner, B. L., Kasperson, R. E., Matson, P. A., McCarthy, J. J., Corell, R. W., Christensen, L., & Martello, M. L. (2003). A framework for vulnerability analysis in sustainability science. *Proceedings of the National Academy of Sciences, 100*(14), 8074–8079.

Vogel, C., & O'Brien, K. (2004). Vulnerability and global environmental change: Rhetoric and reality. *AVISO. Information Bulletin on Global Environmental Change and Human Security, 13*. Retrieved from http://hdl.handle.net/10625/39859

Wisner, P., Blaikie, P., Cannon, T., & Davis, I. (2004). *At risk: Natural hazards, people's vulnerability, and disasters*. London: Routledge.

5   Investing in advanced markets

Motives and determinants

Barbara Jankowska, Anna Matysek-Jędrych

Introduction

The world economy is becoming increasingly global. Developed countries and their firms' role in international trade and investment have been prominent for many years, but developing countries and their companies' position is also increasing. Hence, the direction of investment is now global and multi: from advanced to developing markets, from developing to developing, from advanced to advanced and from developing to advanced markets (see Figure 5.1.). Key debates now focus on whether the existing models, concepts and theories developed mostly based on "First World MNEs" (multinational enterprises) could be applied to explain the decisions of companies from "Third World MNEs".

Motivation for investing in advanced markets

Hymer (1976) clearly demonstrates that firms internationalize when their expected returns derived from their advantage in foreign markets are sufficient to overcome the additional costs and risks associated with operating abroad. Firms expand abroad if they can leverage their ownership advantages thanks to the exploitation of specific host country advantages and their own assets and capabilities. Kim and Aguilera (2016) conducted a broad literature review focused on papers written by location scholars in 1998–2014. However, the authors direct attention not only to location determinants. Nevertheless, it is still a challenge to refer in the discussion just to location determinants in advanced economies.

MNEs select their host countries by considering own motivation to invest abroad. The choice of location is the key aspect in the process of internationalization (Flores & Aguilera, 2007). The characteristics of the host market and neighboring markets play a role. At first, the MNEs must consider *why* they expand abroad and then *where* to expand and invest (Kutschker & Schmid, 2008, p. 377). Thus, subsidiaries are established in locations perceived as attractive from the perspective of the motivation to internationalize (Rugman & Verbeke, 2009, pp. 153–155).

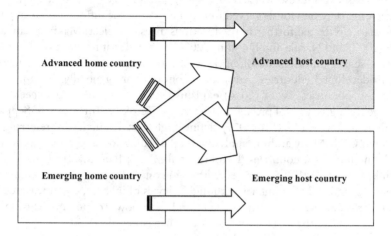

Figure 5.1 Direction of firms' internationalization: global perspective
Source: Own elaboration.

The most popular typology of FDI motives was developed by John Dunning, who distinguished four types (Dunning, 1993, p. 60; Nachum & Zaheer, 2005; Narula & Dunning, 2000):

- (natural) resource-seeking;
- market-seeking;
- efficiency-seeking; and
- strategic asset-seeking.

To be precise, Dunning (1993) proposed a more complete list of motives; however, they have been classified as "other motives:" escape investment, trade-supportive investment, finance-supportive investment, management-supportive investment and passive investment. The model's accessibility and ability to simplify complex ideas into simple and even intuitive concepts made it the foundation for explaining FDI activities. However, the growing complexity of the global economy poses challenges to the explanatory power of this classification.

Resource seekers invest abroad to acquire specific resources that do not exist or exist but at higher costs, in their home country. These resources range from physical ones, like gas and metals, to unskilled and semi-skilled human resources, but also technological and managerial skills. Searching for resources and trying to get access to a bigger market is characteristic of initial investors, of firms that often begin their foreign direct presence. Moreover, entities more experienced in FDI undertake sequential investments and seek opportunities to reduce their costs and access strategic assets (Dunning & Lundan, 2008), i.e., assets that can contribute to their competitive advantage, associated with unique resources and core competences.

Market seekers invest overseas to supply goods or services to new markets or to the ones they previously served through exports. The differences among the motives are reflected further in the locations investors select. Makino, Lau, and Yeh (2002) and Narula and Dunning (2000) revealed that resource-seeking and market-seeking motives are often the two most important motives for investing in developed countries. Advanced economies are generally recognized as high-cost countries. Roos (2016) explains that the level of costs exceeds the average for a given set of production activities. Ketokivi, Turkulainen, Seppala, Rouvinen, and Ali-Yrkko (2017) define high-cost countries by referring to the high GDP. Many authors apply the level of labor cost as the main criterion to define high-cost countries (Ketokivi et al., 2017; Roos, 2016; Yin, Stecke, Swink, & Kaku, 2017). Associated with high costs, advanced economies should also be recognized as countries with higher levels of income, e.g., measured by GDP per capita. Moreover, the greater purchasing power of potential customers may compensate the negative impact of higher labor costs.

Efficiency seekers are driven by the need to rationalize and gain from common governance of geographically dispersed activities through economies of scale and scope or through the benefits of different factor endowments in different countries. Unlike the two previous types of FDI, the motive for strategic asset seekers is less to exploit the advantages firms already possess than to augment existing ones or obtain new ones that contribute to firms' long-term competitiveness. Moreover, efficiency-seeking and strategic asset-seeking are more characteristic of companies that establish their subsidiaries in advanced markets (Dunning, 1993; Nachum & Zaheer, 2005). A strategic asset is often knowledge (Dunning, 1998), so the most relevant locations will be destinations offering access to knowledge and expertise. However, MNEs are motivated by a bundle of factors, which combine the motivations and locations of their investment.

Based on the above considerations, a predominant theoretical approach emerged in the scholarship, which explains the motives of companies investing outside their home market through FDI rather than licensing. The so-called OLI paradigm (ownership-location-internalization) explains the internationalization activity of MNEs, as their attempts to extend ownership advantages to overseas markets by *exploiting* locational advantages – by locating abroad to access low-cost inputs or better serve local markets – and internalizing the efficiency gains from economies of scale and scope by integrating company activities across borders. In short, FDI enables firms to exploit their existing firm-specific assets. This standard explanation seems to have limited application when analyzing the internationalization activity of MNEs from developing countries, as these firms have only limited technological or ownership advantages to exploit. The limited application of Dunning's OLI paradigm was criticized by other economists (cf. Eden & Dai, 2010; Mathews, 2006). However, Dunning himself has repeatedly expressed the conviction that a narrow understanding of the OLI paradigm can indeed lead to wrong conclusions: some MNEs (mostly Third World MNEs) might be prompted to invest in advanced markets to access and augment, rather than to exploit their ownership advantages (Dunning, Narula, & Van Hoesel, 1998, pp. 255–286).

Dominated by the globalization process in which a new set of MNEs from developing markets becomes more prominent, the new environment has raised much debate about the clarifying power of existing theories (Narula, 2012). While opinions continue to differ whether new theories are needed at all (cf. Mathews, 2006), one common view has emerged that differences in country of origin impacts local firm behavior (Cuervo-Cazurra, 2012; Ramamurti, 2009, 2012). This impact is visibly mostly regarding the so-called Third World MNEs, since their firm-specific assets tend to be constrained mostly by the location of home countries (Narula, 2012). Therefore, variations between the internationalization behavior of MNEs from advanced economies and developing markets reflect differences in the locational assets that these MNEs have been able to internalize and turn into firm-specific assets.

However, it seems that the discussion about the motivation of companies to make internationalization decisions focuses on MNEs origin and not on the type of host country. Indeed, regardless of whether the host country is developing or advanced, the four groups of motives defined by Dunning are sufficiently capacious and universal to be considered in the context of both types of host country. In other words, the greater heterogeneity in types of MNEs engaged in cross-border activities does not necessarily mean that there should be more internationalization motives.

Cuervo-Cazurra, Narula, and Un (2015) attempt to clarify the classification of FDI motives by analyzing the MNEs decision through the "double" lens of economics and psychology. The first dimension covers an economics-driven exploration or exploitation of resources, the second − a psychology-driven search for or avoidance of environmental conditions. Such an optics helps to identify four internationalization motives:

- sell more, in which the company exploits existing resources and obtains better host country market conditions;
- buy better, in which the company exploits existing resources abroad and avoids bad home country conditions;
- upgrade, in which the company explores for new resources and obtains better host country conditions; and
- escape, in which the company explores for new resources and avoids bad home country conditions.

At the same time, the above authors argue that their proposal of internationalization motives classification in its nature coincides with the broad outline of motives proposed by Dunning. Therefore, there is direct correspondence between the motives proposed by Dunning and the above team of scientists.

It seems that there is no logical or conceptual reason for the international business scientists to remain bound by the artificial limitation to just four internationalization motives, three of which are based on exploiting company's assets and one that is angled toward exploration of external assets. Indeed, Dunning's concept of internationalization motives can be perceived as a starting point, an eclectic paradigm that provides a toolkit that permits its use in conjunction with other theories and frameworks. Moreover, motivation is always combined with the impact of external and internal factors – the latter related to the firm – which explain why firms choose particular locations for their investment. Referring to Dunning's paradigm, home and host countries provide MNEs with location advantages.

Thus, the location-specific advantages are called country-specific advantages and, as Rugman and Gestrin (1993) claim, they are the "national factor endowments of a nation – basically the variables in its aggregate production function".

Institutional and political determinants of investing abroad: advanced market case

To discover what determines the location of FDI in advanced economies, we may refer to Dunning who distinguished input cost advantages like low wages, the availability of cheap natural resources, labor productivity, market size and character, transport costs, physical distance from home market to potential host markets, barriers to foreign trade, taxation structure, FDI policy and the intensity of rivalry related to the structure of competition. To this bundle of determinants, Dunning and Lundan (2008) added the ability to manage relationships with the host country's institutional environment, which was presented in many studies as the crucial determinant affecting FDI (Alfaro, Kalemli-Ozcan, & Volosovych, 2008; Du, Lu, & Tao, 2008; Fukumi & Nishijima, 2010; Papaioannou, 2009). Other authors (e.g., Jensen et al., 2012) emphasize the importance of institutions to overcome the obsolescing bargain problem identified by Vernon (1971). Different typologies may be applied within the pool of location determinants. We may refer to spheres of the macro environment of firms and additionally distinguish the factors that work at the macro, meso, and micro level.

The broad overview of institutions was provided by North (1981, 1991), who refers to the macro institution and employs the perspective of long-term macroeconomic growth. According to North, institutions are the social, economic, legal and political organizations of the society that support private contracts, protect against expropriation by governments and safeguard from rent-seeking from interest groups. Dixit (2012) indicates that governance structure is defined as the insecurity of property rights and contracts. Thus, the authors often refer to a complex institution which embraces a set of single institutional factors.

Political factors that may lure or push back investors or business partners from specific locations belong to the huge bundle of institutional factors. Political factors may originate in host or home countries. Investors' home country governments may develop incentives for firms to expand into particular directions. For example, Chinese firms are supported by the government to reduce the potential financial burden of these investments (Child & Marinova, 2014; Yeung & Liu, 2008).

There is a broad literature on the political regime (Jensen, 2003; Oneal, 1994), partisanship (Pinto, 2013; Pinto & Pinto, 2008), contractual environment and transaction costs (Henisz, 2000; Henisz & Williamson, 1999), corruption (Caprio, Faccio, & McConnell, 2013; Fredriksson, List, & Millimet, 2003) and FDI flows. Busse and Hefeker (2007, p. 397) manifest with their regression analysis that government stability, internal and external conflict, corruption and ethnic tensions, law and order, democratic accountability and quality of bureaucracy play an important role in location decisions of foreign investors. Some of the factors work as facilitators for FDI inflow and some as inhibitors. For advanced economies, the impact of facilitators like government stability and democratic accountability will be visibly stronger than in the case of less advanced economies, where the impact of inhibitors will be weaker. In the set of institutions important for foreign investors, scholars indicate the property rights institution (PI) and contracting institution (CI) (De Long & Shleifer, 1993; Dixit, 2012; Hart, 1995; North, 1981; Olson, 2000). Private property rights or property protection institution (PI) are more developed in advanced economies since such locations are characterized by strong rules and regulations that protect firms against the power of the government and elite groups. In the case of advanced economies, contracting or contract enforcement institution (CI) is defined as the rules and regulations that protect firms or private individuals against exploitations by one another. Dunning and Lundan (2008) explain that the PI impacts the level of production costs, which means that the strength of PI contributes to the reduction of production costs, which may justify the location of FDI in an advanced economy country. The rights diminish the threat of asset expropriation and property confiscation. The greater the safety of production facilities, warehouses, buildings and machinery in host countries, the greater the attractiveness of the country for FDI. Weak PI is difficult to strengthen in countries where powerful interest groups control policies dedicated to protecting assets (Henisz, 2000), and where foreign firms are not involved in making political and economic decisions in host countries. The existence of PI is a remedy against corrupted authorities and the expropriation of investors who move their assets among countries while conducting FDI.

Locating subsidiaries in a foreign market usually is a long-term investment, hence investors are afraid of changes in government and economic policy. These changes may be even more threatening when the PI is lacking. In advanced economies, the seizure of assets by governments or interest groups, corruption and the expropriation of assets are less likely. Thus, the property rights institution may be recognized as an important determinant of investment in advanced economies.

The contract enforcement institution in the case of advanced economies seems to work better. However, studies reveal that informal networking may be a remedy to contracting institutional constraints (Alcacer & Ingram, 2013; Peng, Sun, Pinkham, & Chen, 2009). Moreover, networking requires a particular level of trust among actors, which is generally higher in the case of advanced countries. CI neutralizes the threat of potential payment failure, shipment delay, quality deterioration and various unprecedented disputes (Antràs & Foley, 2015).

The cost theory points to cost barriers imposed by weak PI and weak CI, which may reduce flows of production assets across countries (Antràs, 2005; Nunn, 2007). However, as Alcacer and Ingram (2013) explain, informal networking may soften institutional cost constraints. Sun, Mellahi, and Thun (2010) present personal networks, business practices or connections, strategic alliances and interpersonal-level embeddedness as solutions to overcome constraints of formal institutions. Furthermore, since network development calls for trust, we may once again assume that it may justify the investment or seeking trade partners in advanced economies. Thus, the institutional features of advanced economies combined with the significance of networking may explain the propensity of investors to locate their businesses in advanced economies, as do companies seeking business partners.

The lack of PI or CI may be a threat for an MNE but according to the obsolescing bargain model, an MNE may simultaneously exploit its bargaining power against host country government by refraining from investment in a particular location. However, after the investment is made, the host country government can change its attitude to the investor and – in the lack of PI – in extreme cases expropriate the assets. Hence, international investors perceive political conditions in host countries as crucial determinants of their location. Thus, "good governance" in advanced economies lures investors and business partners to these locations (Lee, Biglaister, & Staats, 2014). Corruption as a factor of political risk creates costs and uncertainty. Thus, less corruption accompanied by an efficient institutional system results in reduced investment-related transaction costs (Coeurderoy & Murray, 2008; Godinez & Liu, 2015). However, there are studies that present corruption as a factor helping investors to gain the local officials support and acceptance. Lui (1985) reveals bribery to be supportive in bureaucratic processes in the host country; Huntington (1968, p. 61) points to the access corruptions gives to the political elites; and Li and Resnick (2003) express the impact of corruption on the opportunity to deal with host country officials. Moreover, there is empirical support for this alternative view, e.g., Egger and Winner (2005) use panel data to show that – after controlling for confounders – corruption is positively correlated with FDI inflows.

Campos and Kinoshita (2006), Cantwell, Dunning, and Lundan (2010), Castiglione, Gorbunova, Infante, and Smirnova (2012), Gorbunova, Infante, and Smirnova (2012), Peng et al. (2009), Sánchez-Martín, de Arce, and Escribano (2014), Forssbæck and Oxelheim (2008) and Tintin (2013) present that MNEs prefer to establish their businesses in low-risk economies that provide better circumstances for greenfield and acquisitions in which financial factors play the key role.

Some of the institutional factors are related to the technological and knowledge factors, which may be more favorable for advanced economies than for other types of economies. Intellectual property rights protection that is an institutional factor strongly impact the pool of technological and knowledge factors. Wu and Strange (2000) and Javorcik (2004) demonstrated that intellectual property rights protection impacts the location choice of FDI. Du et al. (2008) found that US multinationals prefer to invest in regions with the adequate protection of intellectual property rights, low degree of government intervention in business operations, low level of government corruption and adequate contract enforcement. These features work in the case of advanced economies.

Technological and knowledge factors behind investing in advanced markets

Bearing in mind the peculiarity of advanced economies, we may easily notice that these locations may lure investors who look for technology or even for knowledge. Several years ago, Bhagwati and Srinivasan (1983) and Sun, Tong, and Yu (2002) revealed correlation between FDI flows and investments in scientific research.

The focus on advanced economies as location choices is characteristic of entities often lacking unique capabilities (Cantwell, 1989; Mucchielli & Mayer, 2004). Firms seek not only cheap labor force but also skilled workers that offer particular knowledge. Access to expensive skilled labor force as a determinant of locations choice for FDI works for MNEs that fragment their production processes. They may establish their subsidiaries dedicated to more value adding activities in advanced economies and simple operations based on threshold competencies and resources in countries with lower labor cost. In this way, these MNEs may follow the strategic asset-seeking motivation and not neglect efficiency aspects while conducting FDI. This situation is extremely visible in the case of market-seeking and strategic asset-seeking of Chinese outward FDIs flowing to developed countries across Europe and the United States (Buckley et al., 2007; Cheung & Qian, 2009; De Beule & Duanmu, 2012).

Previous studies indicate that the quality of human capital is more important in service FDI than in manufacturing FDI. Foreign affiliates of service MNEs often reproduce the technologies from their home markets (Blomström & Kokko, 2002). The greater significance of skilled labor combined with economic climate factors for service companies makes advanced economies especially attractive. We simultaneously notice that more advanced economies are more penetrated by services.

High-cost countries are perceived as attractive locations for research activities, and advanced countries are often attractive for firms engaged in continuous innovation (Roos, 2016). Traditionally, advanced economies are recognized as attractive locations for high-end design, product development and R&D operations (Bailey & De Propris, 2014). FDI motivated by strategic assets-seeking directed toward advanced markets is very characteristic of firms from developing markets. In 2004, the UNCTAD World Investment Report presented that foreign investors may be technology-seeking, home-base exploiting and home-base augmenting. Strategic asset-seeking may be linked to "technology-seeking" or "knowledge-seeking". Firms from less developed, developing or even post-transition markets may go abroad in order to improve their home base of R&D – to augment their own assets. In this vein, Chung and Alcácer (2002) indicate that investors sometimes seek knowledge to augment their own assets.

Knowledge-seeking FDI is often associated with developing markets multinationals (EM MNEs; Li, Kong, & Zhang, 2016; Luo & Tung, 2007), while seeking knowledge as a strategic asset is a natural behavior to overcome the "third-world image". Thus, in the case of EM MNEs, the location in an advanced country is a way to overcome this weakness. Ambos, Ambos, and Schlegelmilch (2006) note that the location of a subsidiary in an economically developed – or more developed country than its country of origin – facilitates knowledge transfer from the subsidiary to its parent company. To remove their deficiency in terms of knowledge resources, EM MNEs will invest in Western countries which are more developed in terms of knowledge resources. Moreover, advanced economies are chosen when there are interdependencies between manufacturing and R&D activities (Ketokivi et al., 2017). The location of subsidiaries in advanced markets is determined by the potential opportunity to improve the innovation performance of the parent company or even the whole MNEs corporate network. This determinant works for the situation when foreign firms enter an advanced country but even when advanced country MNEs reshore their production back to their home market (Bailey & De Propris, 2014; Buciuni & Finotto, 2016; Roos, 2016). The opportunity to upgrade the innovation performance of a firm while investing in a more advanced country is determined by the national innovation capacity of the country. The high national innovation capacity is often reflected in higher technological skills and product quality among potentially cooperating companies and entities (Fratocchi, Di Mauro, Barbieri, Nassimbeni, & Zanoni, 2014). Both aspects were indicated by Zhai, Sun, and Zhang (2016) as the determinants of location among firms that are market seekers. Higher technical skills available in advanced countries are sometimes accompanied by greater opportunities to develop capital-intensive production (Yegul, Erenay, Striepe, & Yavuz, 2017). Bearing in mind innovation aspects, we must indicate the significance of knowledge productivity spillovers that emerge thanks to agglomeration, which generates incentives for firms to concentrate in a particular area (Disdier & Mayer, 2004). Agglomeration that leads to positive externalities and economies of scale (Na & Lightfoot, 2006) and its degree is positively correlated with FDI (Braunerhjelm & Svensson, 1996; Coughlin, Terza, & Arromdee, 1991; Wheeler & Mody, 1992). Yu (2013) demonstrates that the availability of other firm's characteristic for the existence of clusters results in more investment in the area. The agglomeration aspect is to some extent related to the aspect of locating FDI in cities. Advanced economies are more penetrated by cities and – as Xu and Yeh (2013) found – FDI tends to favor cities with significant market potential and preferential policies, which may be the next factor luring investors to advanced economies.

The accumulation of knowledge in a location encourages MNEs to establish their entities in a particular area. In the case of advanced economies, quite characteristic is the existence of areas with concentration of R&D affiliates of firms or other R&D institutions. In advanced countries, we may often notice the presence of ecosystems embracing the business, R&D and administration sectors. These ecosystems contribute much to the knowledge creation and dissemination, and they are conducive to knowledge spillovers; they are often spatially concentrated and function as business clusters. The development of clusters is often higher in more advanced economies, since the strength of business clusters often accompanies the level of economic development. Thus, firms investing in advanced countries or having business partners from these countries receive greater opportunities to take advantage from being a cluster firm. The characteristic feature of successful clusters is the diffusion of knowledge as noticed more than 20 years ago by Baptista and Swann (1998), and it remains valid. Many studies indicate the significance of knowledge management in clusters (e.g., Ciravegna, 2011; Rabellotti & Morrison, 2009). Clusters that enjoy a good reputation, high status and legitimacy spillovers greatly contribute to the perception of the entities that operate in these clusters, and this positive perception contributes to the reputation, status and legitimacy of the clusters (Ferreira, Serra, Kramer Costa, Maccari, & Couto, 2012; Porter, 1998). Nevertheless, access to these advantages of clusters and opportunities to capture these advantages is more probable in more advanced economies that are more penetrated by business clusters. Thus, a determinant to locate the subsidiary in an advanced economy may be the greater opportunities to tap into clusters.

Knowledge-seeking and technology-seeking investors will choose advanced economies since they are characterized by higher national innovation capacity, which has been presented many times in the Global Innovation Index in the Global Competitiveness Report. Thus, the factors that contribute to a national innovation capacity and determine its level may work as facilitators of FDI inflow to these economies. Advanced economies are characterized by not only a higher level of innovation but by an environment for innovation. It means that the determinants of subsidiary location in an advanced economy may be the size of scientific and technical labor force, incentives for private firms to get involved in R&D and the development and productivity of the R&D public sector in the country. Broadly speaking, the innovation infrastructure embracing the human and financial resources a country dedicated to innovation, public policy measures devoted to innovative activity and the level of technological sophistication of the economy may lure foreign firms to advanced economies. In advanced economies, access to professionals in the R&D sector is easier because the pool of scientist and engineers is larger. As these economies are generally richer, they are characterized by a developed sector of basic research that may further facilitate commercial technology. The presence of R&D institutions is accompanied by legal regulations that contribute to the national innovation capacity because the legal factors consist of intellectual property, tax-based measures to foster innovation and antitrust policies that promote innovation-based competition.

Firms seeking the improvement of efficiency look for locations that improve their lead time and effectiveness to customer response. In this case, what may play a key role is not the innovation infrastructure but the general infrastructure, especially related to transportation and communication. Infrastructure as a factor that lures foreign investors appears in many previous studies about developing countries (e.g., Alguacil, Cuadros, & Orts, 2011; Campos & Kinoshita, 2006; Gorbunova et al., 2012). Graf and Mudambi (2005) highlight that the importance of infrastructure greatly depends on the specificity of an industry: whether it is manufacturing or services. Nevertheless, we may assume that the quality and availability of infrastructure in advanced economies makes their locations more attractive than other groups of countries. Another aspect is the perception of products by customers who associate high-cost countries with higher quality, and the made-in effect is crucial (Di Mauro, Fratocchi, Orzes, & Sartor, 2018).

Globalization drivers versus firms' expansion into advanced countries

There are many challenges to discuss all the determinants and motives of companies' investment into advanced markets. It is nearly impossible to fully systematize knowledge on this subject. Therefore, researchers often refer to existing models that comprehensively analyze an alternative phenomenon, which simultaneously indirectly helps to explain another phenomenon in the political-economic or business environment. We also apply such a procedure was applied in this book.

In order to consider the different factors and motives that determine companies' decisions to invest in advanced markets – as consistently and comprehensively as possible – we reference the Yip (1996, 2000, 2004) model, which identifies four groups of drivers of contemporary globalization process (cf. Table 5.1). Interestingly, the author himself considers these drivers to be variables determining companies' behaviors and decisions to create a strategy in the global dimension and to expand their participation in foreign markets. Thus, these drivers can nearly by nature be considered proxies for both motives and determinants of companies' expansion. The approach proposed by Yip (1996, 2004) undoubtedly facilitates the operationalization of the variables used in empirical research (see Chapter 7).

Along with dynamic technological development, Yip (2000, 2004) reviews the proposed industry drivers of globalization by supplementing them with those directly resulting from the use of the Internet in businesses. Based on research, Yip (2000, 2004) concludes that the widespread use of the Internet will intensify the globalization potential of companies, influencing the drivers from all four categories: market, cost, governmental and competitive. Therefore, we may expect that the expansion of companies into host markets will be an increasingly common phenomenon in the business environment.

Table 5.1 Industry globalization drivers according to Yip

Driver category	Driver description
Market drivers	• Homogenous customer makes participation in many markets easier • Global customers: the existence of such customers forces companies to create global account management • Global channels create an opportunity for rationalizing worldwide pricing
Cost drivers	• Economies of scale and scope: both economies can be increased through participation in multiple markets • Learning and experiencing: expanded market participation can accelerate the accumulation of learning and experience • Sourcing efficiencies: centralized purchasing in multiple markets can significantly lower costs • Favorable logistics: low transportation costs enhance companies' ability to concentrate production
Governmental drivers	• Favorable trade policies: liberal trade policies enhance companies' ability to expand • Compatible technical standards: reducing differences in technical standards promotes product standardization in many markets • Common Marketing regulations: similar regulations for marketing activities allows for the unification of the global marketing approach
Competitive drivers	• Interdependence of countries: a company can create competitive relationship between markets by implementing a global strategy, forcing other companies to follow such a strategy and intensify their expansion activities • Globalized competitors: the pursuit of overtaking global competitors can increase the scale of expansion into new markets

Source: Own elaboration based on Yip (1992, 1996, 2000, 2013).

Concluding remarks

The expansion of companies into foreign markets is not something new. For many years, companies have more-or-less successfully attempted to "conquer" host markets. Initially, researchers investigated the phenomenon of internationalization and focused on MNEs from developed countries and their expansion into developing markets. This was a status quo in the arrangement of business forces around the world.

The "saturation" of developing markets with First World MNEs and the dynamic development of Third World MNEs made advanced markets gain popularity as the direction of investment and expansion. Such a phenomenon automatically raised questions about the causes, determinants and motivations underlying companies' decisions to expand into advanced markets.

Regardless of the methodology or model used to identify the factors determining or motivating companies to expand into new markets – especially in advanced countries – what arises most often is the issue of broadly understood market attractiveness. This attractiveness may be costs-related, resources-related (natural, strategic, knowledge and innovation) or efficiency-related. Due to institutional arrangements, the British market is a specific European market. Companies that decide to expand into this market must consider the dynamics and unpredictability of the rules that will apply in the post-Brexit period (see Chapters 6 and 8).

References

Alcacer, J., & Ingram, P. (2013). Spanning the institutional abyss: The intergovernmental network and the governance of foreign direct investment. *American Journal of Sociology, 118*(4), 1055–1098. https://doi.org/10.1086/668692

Alfaro, L., Kalemli-Ozcan, S., & Volosovych, V. (2008). Why doesn't capital flow from rich to poor countries? An empirical investigation. *The Review of Economics and Statistics, 90*(2), 347–368. Retrieved from www.jstor.org/stable/40043150

Alguacil, M., Cuadros, A., & Orts, V. (2011). Inward FDI and growth: The role of macroeconomic and institutional environment. *Journal of Policy Modelling, 33*(3), 481–496. https://doi.org/10.1016/j.jpolmod.2010.12.004

Ambos, T. C., Ambos, B., & Schlegelmilch, B. B. (2006). Learning from foreign subsidiaries: An empirical investigation of headquarters' benefits from reverse knowledge transfers. *International Business Review, 15*(3), 294–312. https://doi.org/10.1016/j.ibusrev.2006.01.002

Antràs, P. (2005). Incomplete contracts and the product cycle. *American Economic Review, 95*(4), 1054–1073. https://doi.org/10.1257/0002828054825600

Antràs, P., & Foley, C. F. (2015). Poultry in motion: A study of international trade finance practices. *Journal of Political Economy, 123*(4), 853–901. https://doi.org/10.1086/681592

Bailey, D., & De Propris, L. (2014). Manufacturing reshoring and its limits: The UK automotive case. *Cambridge Journal of Regions, Economy and Society, 7*(3), 379–395. https://doi.org/10.1093/cjres/rsu019

Baptista, R., & Swann, G. M. P. (1998). Do firms in clusters innovate more? *Research Policy, 27*(5), 525–540. https://doi.org/10.1016/S0048-7333(98)00065-1

Bhagwati, J. N., & Srinivasan, T. N. (1983). *Lectures in international trade.* Cambridge, MA: MIT Press.

Blomström, M. A., & Kokko, A. (2002). *FDI and human capital: A research agenda.* OECD Development Centre Working Paper 195. https://doi.org/10.1787/18151949

Braunerhjelm, P., & Svensson, R. (1996). Host country characteristics and agglomeration in foreign direct investment. *Applied Economics, 28*(7), 833–840. https://doi.org/10.1080/000368496328272

Buciuni, G., & Finotto, V. (2016). Innovation in global value chains: Co-location of production and development in Italian low-tech industries. *Regional Studies, 50*(12), 2010–2023. https://doi.org/10.1080/00343404.2015.1115010

Buckley, P. J., Clegg, L., Cross, A., Liu, X., Voss, H., & Zheng, P. (2007). The determinants of Chinese outward foreign direct investment. *Journal of International Business Studies, 38*(4), 499–518. https://doi.org/10.1016/j.ememar.2011.06.001

Busse, M., & Hefeker, C. (2007). Political risk, institutions and foreign direct investment. *European Journal of Political Economy, 23*(2), 397–415. https://doi.org/10.1016/j.ejpoleco.2006.02.003

Campos, N. F., & Kinoshita, Y. (2006). Determinants and effects of foreign direct investment in transition economies. In J. Nakagawa (Ed.), *Managing development: Globalization, economic restructuring and social policy.* London: Routledge.

Cantwell, J. (1989). *Technological innovation and multinational corporations.* Cambridge, MA: Basil Blackwell.

Cantwell, J., Dunning, J. H., & Lundan, S. M. (2010). An evolutionary approach to understanding international business activity: The co-evolution of MNEs and the institutional environment. *Journal of International Business Studies, 41*(4), 567–586. https://doi.org/10.1057/jibs.2009.95

Caprio, L., Faccio, M., & McConnell, J. J. (2013). Sheltering corporate assets from political extraction. *Journal of Law, Economics, and Organization, 29*(2), 332–354. https://doi.org/10.1093/jleo/ewr018

Castiglione, C., Gorbunova, Y., Infante, D., & Smirnova, J. (2012). FDI determinants in an idiosyncratic country. A reappraisal over the Russian regions during transition years. *Communist and Post-Communist Studies, 45*(1–2), 1–10. https://doi.org/10.1016/j.postcomstud.2012.02.006

Cheung, Y.-W., & Qian, X. (2009). Empirics of China's outward direct investment. *Pacific Economic Review, 14*(3), 312–341. https://doi.org/10.1111/j.1468-0106.2009.00451.x

Child, J., & Marinova, S. (2014). The role of contextual combinations in the globalization of Chinese firms. *Management and Organization Review, 10*(3), 347–371. https://doi.org/10.1017/S1740877600004289

Chung, W., & Alcácer, J. (2002). Knowledge seeking and location choice of foreign direct investment in the United States. *Management Science, 48*(12), 1534–1554. https://doi.org/10.1287/mnsc.48.12.1534.440

Ciravegna, L. (2011). FDI, social ties and technological learning in new Silicon Valley clones. Evidence from the Costa Rican ICT cluster. *Journal of Development Studies, 47*(8), 1178–1198. https://doi.org/10.1080/00220388.2010.547935

Coeurderoy, R., & Murray, G. (2008). Regulatory environments and the location decision: Evidence from the early foreign market entries of new-technology-based firms. *Journal of International Business Studies, 39*(4), 670–687. https://doi.org/10.1057/palgrave.jibs.8400369

Coughlin, C., Terza, J., & Arromdee, V. (1991). State characteristics and the location of foreign direct investment within the United States. *The Review of Economics and Statistics, 73*(4), 675–683. Retrieved from www.jstor.org/stable/2109406

Cuervo-Cazurra, A. (2012). Extending theory by analyzing developing country multinational companies: Solving the Goldilocks debate. *Global Strategy Journal, 2*(3), 153–167. https://doi.org/10.1111/j.2042-5805.2012.01039.x

Cuervo-Cazurra, A., Narula, R., & Un, C. A. (2015). Internationalization motives: Sell more, buy better, upgrade and escape. *Multinational Business Review, 23*(1), 25–35. https://doi.org/10.1108/MBR-02-2015-0009

De Beule, F., & Duanmu, J.-L. (2012). Locational determinants of internationalization: A firm level analysis of Chinese and Indian acquisitions. *European Management Journal, 30*(3), 264–277. https://doi.org/10.1016/j.emj.2012.03.006

De Long, J. B., & Shleifer, A. (1993). Princes and merchants: European city growth before the industrial revolution. *The Journal of Law and Economics, 36*(2), 671–702. https://doi.org/10.1086/467294

Di Mauro, C., Fratocchi, L., Orzes, G., & Sartor, M. (2018). Offshoring and backshoring: A multiple case study analysis. *Journal of Purchasing and Supply Management, 24*(2), 108–134. https://doi.org/10.1016/j.pursup.2017.07.003

Disdier, A.-C., & Mayer, T. (2004). How different is Eastern Europe? Structure and determinants of location choices by French firms in Eastern and Western Europe. *Journal of Comparative Economics, 32*(2), 280–296. https://doi.org/10.1016/j.jce.2004.02.004

Dixit, A. (2012). *Governance, development and foreign direct investment*. Max Weber Program. Italy: The European University Institute.

Du, J., Lu, Y., & Tao, Z. (2008). Economic institutions and FDI location choice: Evidence from US multinationals in China. *Journal of Comparative Economics*, *36*(3), 412–429. https://doi.org/10.1016/j.jce.2008.04.004

Dunning, J. H. (1993). *Multinational enterprises and the global economy*. New York: Addison Wesley.

Dunning, J. H. (1998). Location and the multinational enterprise: A neglected factor? *Journal of International Business Studies*, *29*, 45–66. https://doi.org/10.1057/palgrave.jibs.8490024

Dunning, J. H., & Lundan, S. (2008). *Multinational enterprises and the global economy*. Cheltenham: Edward Elgar Publishing.

Dunning, J. H., Narula, R., & Van Hoesel, R. (1998). Third world multinationals revisited: New developments and theoretical implications. In J. H. Dunning (Ed.), *Globalisation, trade and foreign direct investment* (pp. 255–286). Oxford: Elsevier.

Eden, L., & Dai, L. (2010). Rethinking the O in Dunning's OLI/Eclectic paradigm. *The Multinational Business Review*, *18*(1), 13–34. https://doi.org/doi.org/10.1108/1525383X201000008

Egger, P., & Winner, H. (2005). Evidence on corruption as an incentive for foreign direct investment. *European Journal of Political Economy*, *21*(4), 932–952. https://doi.org/10.1016/j.ejpoleco.2005.01.002

Ferreira, M. P., Serra, F. R., Kramer Costa, B., Maccari, E., & Couto, H. R. (2012). Impact of the types of clusters on the innovation output and the appropriation of rents from innovation. *Journal of Technology Management and Innovation*, *7*(4), 70–80. https://doi.org/10.4067/S0718-27242012000400006

Flores, R., & Aguilera, R. V. (2007). Globalization and location choice: An analysis of US multinational firms in 1980 and 2000. *Journal of International Business Studies*, *38*(7), 1187–1210. https://doi.org/10.1057/palgrave.jibs.8400307

Forssbæck, J., & Oxelheim, L. (2008). Finance-specific factors as drivers of cross-border investment – An empirical investigation. *International Business Review*, *17*(6), 630–641. https://doi.org/10.1016/j.ibusrev.2008.09.001

Fratocchi, L., Di Mauro, C., Barbieri, P., Nassimbeni, G., & Zanoni, A. (2014). When manufacturing moves back: Concepts and questions. *Journal of Purchasing and Supply Management*, *20*(1), 54–59. https://doi.org/10.1016/j.pursup.2014.01.004

Fredriksson, P. G., List, J. A., & Millimet, D. L. (2003). Bureaucratic corruption, environmental policy and inbound US FDI: Theory and evidence. *Journal of Public Economics*, *87*(7–8), 1407–1430. https://doi.org/10.1016/S0047-2727(02)00016-6

Fukumi, A., & Nishijima, S. (2010). Institutional quality and foreign direct investment in Latin America and the Caribbean. *Applied Economics*, *42*(14), 1857–1864. https://doi.org/10.1080/00036840701748979

Godinez, J. R., & Liu, L. (2015). Corruption distance and FDI flows into Latin America. *International Business Review*, *24*(1), 33–42. https://doi.org/10.1016/j.ibusrev.2014.05.006

Gorbunova, Y., Infante, D., & Smirnova, J. (2012). New evidences on FDI determinants. An appraisal over the transition period. *Prague Economic Papers*, *21*(2), 129–149. https://doi.org/10.18267/j.pep.415

Graf, M., & Mudambi, S. M. (2005). The outsourcing of IT-enabled business processes: A conceptual model of the location decision. *Journal of International Management*, *11*(2), 253–268. https://doi.org/10.1016/j.intman.2005.03.010

Hart, O. (1995). *Firms, contracts and financial structure*. Oxford: Oxford University Press.

Henisz, W. J. (2000). The institutional environment for multinational investment. *Journal of Law, Economics, and Organization, 16*(2), 334–364. https://doi.org/10.1093/jleo/16.2.334

Henisz, W. J., & Williamson, O. E. (1999). Comparative economic organization – Within and between countries. *Business & Politics, 1*(3), 261–278. https://doi.org/10.1515/bap.1999.1.3.261

Huntington, S. P. (1968). *Political order in changing societies*. New Haven, CT: Yale University Press.

Hymer, S. H. (1976). *The international operations of national firms: A study of direct foreign investment*. Cambridge, MA: MIT Press.

Javorcik, B. S. (2004). The composition of foreign direct investment and protection of intellectual property rights: Evidence from transition economies. *European Economic Review, 48*(1), 39–62. https://doi.org/10.1016/S0014-2921(02)00257-X

Jensen, N. M. (2003). Democratic governance and multinational corporations: Political regimes and inflows of foreign direct investment. *International Organization, 57*(3), 587–616. https://doi.org/10.1017/S0020818303573040

Jensen, N. M., Biglaiser, G., Li, Q., Malesky, E., Pinto, P. M., Pinto, S. M., & Staats, J. L. (2012). *Politics and foreign direct investment*. Ann Arbor, MI: University of Michigan Press.

Ketokivi, M., Turkulainen, V., Seppala, T., Rouvinen, P., & Ali-Yrkko, J. (2017). Why locate manufacturing in a high-cost country? A case study of 35 production location decisions. *Journal of Operations Management, 49–51*, 20–30. https://doi.org/10.1016/j.jom.2016.12.005

Kim, J. U., & Aguilera, R. V. (2016). Foreign location choice: Review and extensions. *International Journal of Management Reviews, 18*(2), 133–159. https://doi.org/10.1111/ijmr.12064

Kutschker, N., & Schmid, S. (2008). *Internationales management (International management)*. Munich: Oldenbourg.

Lee, H., Biglaister, G., & Staats, J. L. (2014). The effects of political risk on different entry modes of foreign direct investment. *International Interactions, 40*(5), 683–710. https://doi.org/10.1080/03050629.2014.899225

Li, Q., & Resnick, A. (2003). Reversal of fortunes: Democratic institutions and foreign direct investment inflows to developing countries. *International Organization, 57*(1), 175–211. https://doi.org/10.1017/S0020818303571077

Li, Y. S., Kong, X. X., & Zhang, M. (2016). Industrial upgrading in global production networks: The case of the Chinese automotive industry. *Asia Pacific Business Review, 22*(1), 21–37. https://doi.org/10.1080/13602381.2014.990203

Lui, F. T. (1985). An equilibrium queuing model of bribery. *Journal of Political Economy, 93*(4), 760–781. Retrieved from www.jstor.org/stable/1832136

Luo, Y., & Tung, R. (2007). International expansion of emerging market enterprises: A springboard perspective. *Journal of International Business Studies, 38*(4), 481–498. https://doi.org/10.1057/palgrave.jibs.8400275

Makino, S., Lau, Ch.-M., & Yeh, R.-S. (2002). Asset-exploitation versus asset-seeking: Implications for location choice of foreign direct investment from newly industrialized economies. *Journal of International Business Studies, 33*(3), 403–421. https://doi.org/10.1057/palgrave.jibs.8491024

Mathews, J. A. (2006). Dragon multinationals: New players in 21st century globalization. *Asia Pacific Journal of Management, 23*(1), 5–27. https://doi.org/10.1007/s10490-006-6113-0

Mucchielli, J.-L., & Mayer, T. (2004). *Multinational firms' location and the new economic geography*. Cheltenham: Edward Elgar Publishing. https://doi.org/10.4337/9781845420628.00001

Na, L., & Lightfoot, W. S. (2006). Determinants of foreign direct investment at the regional level in China. *Journal of Technology Management in China*, 1(3), 262–278. https://doi.org/10.1108/17468770610704930

Nachum, L., & Zaheer, S. (2005). The persistence of distance? The impact of technology on MNE motivations for foreign investment. *Strategic Management Journal*, 26(8), 747–767. https://doi.org/10.1002/smj.472

Narula, R. (2012). Do we need different frameworks to explain infant MNEs from developing countries? *Global Strategy Journal*, 2(3), 188–204. https://doi.org/10.1111/j.2042-5805.2012.01035.x

Narula, R., & Dunning, J. H. (2000). Industrial development, globalization and multinational enterprises: New realities for developing countries. *Oxford Development Studies*, 28(2), 141–167. https://doi.org/10.1080/713688313

North, D. C. (1981). *Structure and change in economic history*. New York: Norton.

North, D. C. (1991). Institutions. *Journal of Economic Perspectives*, 5(1), 97–112. https://doi.org/10.1257/jep.5.1.97

Nunn, N. (2007). Relationship-specificity, incomplete contracts, and the pattern of trade. *The Quarterly Journal of Economics*, 122(2), 569–600. https://doi.org/10.1162/qjec.122.2.569

Olson, M. (2000). *Power and prosperity: Outgrowing communist and capitalist dictatorships*. Oxford: Oxford University Press.

Oneal, J. R. (1994). The affinity of foreign investors for authoritarian regimes. *Political Research Quarterly*, 47(3), 565–588. https://doi.org/10.1177/106591299404700302

Papaioannou, E. (2009). What drives international financial flows? Politics, institutions and other determinants. *Journal of Development Economics*, 88(2), 269–281. https://doi.org/10.1016/j.jdeveco.2008.04.001

Peng, M., Sun, S. L., Pinkham, B., & Chen, H. (2009). The institution-based view as a third leg for a strategy tripod. *Academy of Management Perspectives*, 23(3), 63–81. https://doi.org/10.5465/AMP.2009.43479264

Pinto, P. M. (2013). *Partisan investment in the global economy: Why the left loves foreign direct investment and FDI loves the left*. Cambridge & New York: Cambridge University Press.

Pinto, P. M., & Pinto, S. M. (2008). The politics of investment: Partisanship and the sectoral allocation of foreign direct investment. *Economics & Politics*, 20(2), 216–254. https://doi.org/10.1111/j.1468-0343.2008.00330.x

Porter, M. E. (1998). Clusters and new economics of competition. *Harvard Business Review*. Retrieved from https://hbr.org/1998/11/clusters-and-the-new-economics-of-competition

Rabellotti, R., & Morrison, A. (2009). Knowledge and information networks in an Italian wine cluster. *European Planning Studies*, 17(7), 983–1006. https://doi.org/10.1080/09654310902949265

Ramamurti, R. (2009). What have we learned about emerging-market MNEs? In R. Ramamurti & J. V. Singh (Eds.), *Emerging multinationals in emerging markets* (pp. 399–426). Cambridge: Cambridge University Press.

Ramamurti, R. (2012). What is really different about emerging market multinationals? *Global Strategy Journal*, 2(1), 41–47. https://doi.org/10.1002/gsj.1025

Roos, G. (2016). Design-based innovation for manufacturing firm success in high-cost operating environments. *The Journal of Design, Economics, and Innovation*, 2(1), 5–28. https://doi.org/10.1016/j.sheji.2016.03.001

Rugman, A. M., & Gestrin, M. (1993). The strategic response of multinational enterprises to NAFTA. *The Columbia Journal of World Business, 28*(4), 18–29. https://doi.org/10.1016/0022-5428(93)90002-7

Rugman, S. M., & Verbeke, A. (2009). Location, competitiveness, and the multinational enterprise. In S. M. Rugman (Ed.), *The Oxford handbook of international business.* Oxford: Oxford Publishing. https://doi.org/10.1093/oxfordhb/9780199234257.001.0001

Sánchez-Martín, M. E., de Arce, R., & Escribano, G. (2014). Do changes in the rules of the game affect FDI flows in Latin America? A look at the macroeconomic, institutional and regional integration determinants of FDI. *European Journal of Political Economy, 34,* 279–299. https://doi.org/10.1016/j.ejpoleco.2014.02.001

Sun, P., Mellahi, K., & Thun, E. (2010). The dynamic value of MNE political embeddedness: The case of the Chinese automobile industry. *Journal of International Business Studies, 41,* 1161–1182. https://doi.org/10.1057/jibs.2009.94

Sun, Q., Tong, W., & Yu, Q. (2002). Determinants of foreign direct investment across China. *Journal of International Money and Finance, 21,* 79–113. https://doi.org/10.1016/S0261-5606(01)00032-8

Tintin, C. (2013). The determinants of foreign direct investment inflows in the Central and Eastern European countries: The importance of institutions. *Communist and Post-Communist Studies, 46*(2), 287–298. https://doi.org/10.1016/j.postcomstud.2013.03.006

Vernon, R. (1971). *Sovereignty at bay: The multinational spread of U.S. enterprises.* New York: Basic Books.

Wheeler, D., & Mody, A. (1992). International investment location decisions: The case of U.S. firms. *Journal of International Economics, 33*(1–2), 57–76. https://doi.org/10.1016/0022-1996(92)90050-T

Wu, X., & Strange, R. (2000). The location of foreign insurance companies in China. *International Business Review, 9*(3), 383–398. https://doi.org/10.1016/S0969-5931(00)00007-X

Xu, Z., & Yeh, A. (2013). Origin effects, spatial dynamics and redistribution of FDI in guangdong, China. *Tijdschrift Voor Economische En Sociale Geografie, 104*(4), 439–455. https://doi.org/10.1111/tesg.2013.104.issue-4

Yegul, M. F., Erenay, F. S., Striepe, S., & Yavuz, M. (2017). Improving configuration of complex production lines via simulation-based optimization. *Computers and Industrial Engineering, 109,* 295–312. https://doi.org/10.1016/j.cie.2017.04.019

Yeung, H. W.-C., & Liu, W. (2008). Globalizing China: The rise of mainland Chinese firms in the global economy. *Eurasian Geography and Economics, 49*(1), 57–86. https://doi.org/10.2747/1539-7216.49.1.57

Yin, Y., Stecke, K. E., Swink, M., & Kaku, I. (2017). Lessons from seru production on manufacturing competitively in a high cost environment. *Journal of Operations Management, 49–51,* 67–76. https://doi.org/10.1016/j.jom.2017.01.003

Yip, G. (1992). *Total global strategy.* Englewood Cliffs, NJ: Prentice Hall.

Yip, G. (1996). Global strategy as a factor in Japanese success. *Thunderbird International Business Review, 38*(1), 145–167. https://doi.org/10.1002/tie.5060380111

Yip, G. (2000). Global strategy in the internet era. *Business Strategy Review, 11*(4), 1–14. https://doi.org/10.1111/1467-8616.00152

Yip, G. (2004). Using strategy to change your business model. *Business Strategy Review, 15*(2), 17–24. https://doi.org/10.1111/j.0955-6419.2004.00308.x

Yip, G. (2013). *Total global strategy.* London: Pearson Education.

Yu, P. (2013). Heterogeneity of foreign R&D affiliates location strategies in China: An analysis based on industrial cluster theory. *Economic Review*, 6. Retrieved from https://en.cnki.com.cn/Article_en/CJFDTotal-JJPL201306010.htm

Zhai, W., Sun, S., & Zhang, G. (2016). Reshoring of American manufacturing companies from China. *Operations Management Research*, 9(3–4), 62–74. https://doi.org/10.1007/s12063-016-0114-z

6 FDI as a key form of economies' internationalization

Szymon Bytniewski, Marlena Dzikowska,
Jan Polowczyk

Introduction

The EU enabled the creation of an internal market, which in a short period of time intensified the internationalization processes of companies operating within the EU territory and contributed to an increase in the volume of trade between EU member states. The unification of trade exchange terms created favorable conditions for internationalization. The internationalization process in the EU market may be described as the "foreign economic activity of companies operating in the uniform area of the internal market" (Wiktor, 2005). The international activity of companies in the EU territory is rather peculiar, because the liberalization and unification of the market enables the companies to conduct their activity in a similar or identical manner as on home markets. In certain cases, such as the UK, it is impossible to replicate the methods used on home markets. Companies must consider differences in the economic or sociocultural sphere. The need to adapt the internationalization process may be determined by such factors as state wealth, consumer purchasing power and cultural differences.

FDI: developed and developing countries

The riskiest forms of economic activity internationalization, which at the same time give a chance to achieve a high level of control, include FDI. According to the definition of the UNCTAD, FDI is a category of international investment made by a resident of one country ("direct investor" or "parent company") with the intention of exercising long-term control over a company of another country ("subsidiary"). For an investment to be considered FDI, the minimum threshold of direct investor's capital engagement in the direct investment enterprise is set at 10%.

Based on statistics from the past three decades, we may notice the growing importance of FDI in the global economy (Figure 6.1). Moreover, we also witness an increase in the share of developing countries in the global FDI pool. In 2019, over 44% of almost USD 1.5 trillion of global FDI flows were directed to developing countries, providing much needed private capital. For many developing countries, FDI became the main source of external financing.

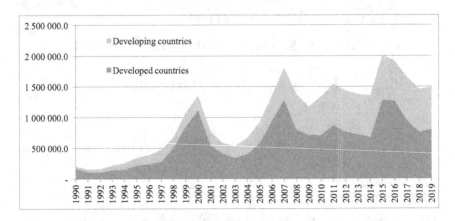

Figure 6.1 FDI divided into developed and developing countries, 1990–2019, in millions of USD

Source: UNCTAD (2020).

There are many theories in science that explain the significance of FDI inflow. In the traditional perspective, FDI is explained as a capital flow related to differences in investment returns between countries. Neoclassical economists consider the inflow of foreign capital a source of economic development and openness to other economies. Moreover, FDI increase the prospects for raising living standards. They not only serve to transfer capital but also provide various forms of international support for local companies involving the transfer of intangible assets, including technologies, business techniques and qualified workers (Levin, 2001).

Dunning and Lundan (2008) present a theory called the "OLI paradigm," which explains why companies invest abroad. According to the OLI paradigm, an FDI occurs when there exist specific advantages of Ownership, such as own technology, combined with the advantages resulting from Location, such as low factor costs, along with potential benefits of Internationalization, i.e., locating the production process abroad.

The objectives of FDI inflow to the host country may be divided into various categories, e.g., gaining access to natural resources and consumer markets, using comparative advantage at the location level and participation in R&D. There exist many studies on the reasons for FDI in the literature but no consensus has been reached so far (Kok & Acikgoz Ersoy, 2009). Various concepts are based on different assumptions and set of indicators (Azam & Lukman, 2010; Greene & Villanueva, 1991; Miskinis & Juozenaite, 2015; Singhania & Gupta, 2011), which are sensitive to specific conditions and locations, resulting in the inability to generalize the results.

Scholars established that labor costs, tax systems, R&D activities or GDP dynamics can affect FDI both negatively and positively, depending on the economic and political outlook of the host country. Moreover, the literature postulates the potential determinants of FDI and classifies them as economic, political and institutional factors. Among other things, the economic factors include trade openness, exchange rate, infrastructure and market size (Alam & Zulfiqar Ali Shah, 2013; Leitão & Faustino, 2010; Masuku & Dlamini, 2009). The political factors consist of political stability, government effectiveness, the quality of legal regulations and the level of corruption (Asiedu & Lien, 2004; Mina, 2009), whereas the institutional factors comprise a rich set of interdependent factors, and the basic measure of the institutional environment is the level of "economic freedom" enjoyed by investors in the host country (Asiedu, 2006; Bevan, Estrin, & Meyer, 2004; Henisz & Swaminathan, 2008).

Considering the three categories of factors, Saini and Singhania (2018) describe differences in the factors influencing FDI in developed and developing countries. They divide the causes of FDI into three types: market-seeking, seeking cheaper resources to reduce costs and seeking assets related to strategy implementation. Saini and Singhania (2018) state that in developed countries the key determinants of FDI relate to macroeconomic and political elements – GDP growth, trade openness and freedom index – while in developing countries FDI shows a positive connection with economic factors: market size and operating costs.

Foreign capital flows influence the growth process of both developed and developing countries. Developed countries need foreign capital inflows for sustainable development – the development of environmental technologies – while developing countries need them for growth and investment (Piteli, 2010; Saini & Singhania, 2018).

FDI increases income and total factor productivity (TFP) (Li & Liu, 2005; Woo, 2009), because they are considered the source of technological diffusion, which in turn leads to economic growth and higher living standards (Apergis, Economidou, & Filippidis, 2008; Chang & Luh, 2000; Xiaming, Parker, Kirit, & Yingqi, 2001; Zhang, 2002). To benefit from technological diffusion, a country must be advanced enough to absorb innovative technology. Developed countries absorb technological progress faster than developing countries.

The latest empirical data largely confirm the above research results. *Global Investment Competitiveness Survey 2017–2018* (World Bank, 2018) presents the results of interviews with 754 directors of MNEs. The study shows how MNEs decide on FDI and select target countries. Moreover, the study presents operational experiences, reinvestments and MNEs' expansions, along with their reactions to political risks and decisions to close down foreign subsidiaries. The study uses the scheme proposed by Dunning and Lundan (2008), which distinguishes four sources of motivation for FDI: natural resources in the host country, access to the host country's market, strategic assets in the host market and cost reduction through higher production efficiency.

MNEs primarily seek access to natural resources and are most interested in such factors as access to land and resources, e.g., oil, gas, forests and agricultural products. The size and purchasing power of the host country's internal market remains crucial for FDI in search of sales markets. In turn, corporations focused on investing in strategic assets primarily seek technologies and brands that can improve their operations and strengthen their competitiveness. Meanwhile, FDI focused on the pursuit of efficiency seek countries with cheaper production factors, which are conducive to lowering production costs. Moreover, FDI seeking to optimize effectiveness include corporations that participate in global value chains (GVCs).

The four types of investment strategies may react differently to different political conditions and the general investment climate. Investors seeking access to natural resources, strategic assets and market investments usually are less sensitive to changes in the investment climate, provided they can find resources to exploit in the host county, an enterprise with competitive advantage, or if the local market offers attractive opportunities. On the other hand, the investors focused on enhancing efficiency – whose investment decisions are largely dictated by cost-cutting – are usually very sensitive to any factors that increase their operating costs or hinder the free exchange of goods and services with the rest of the world in global networks.

The aforementioned *GIC Survey 2017–2018* presents results on investors who target developing countries and were asked about their motives for investment activities. The survey results are presented in Table 6.1.

The percentages on the right side of Table 6.1 do not add up to 100% because the responders could choose multiple motivations: 62% of the respondents chose two or more answers. Many respondents could have interpreted the motivation to access new sales markets or clients as not only access to a host country market but also to a regional market. In reality, this motivation was often selected in the case of FDI in small developing countries with an extensive network of trade and investment agreements with other economies, which suggests that the respondents were interested in accessing new regional markets or regional consumers and not just the small local market of the host country.

Elaborating the above considerations, we may compare the motives of investors engaged in FDI by dividing per developed and developing countries. Such a comparison is presented in Table 6.2.

The benefits of FDI far exceed attracting the necessary capital. FDI also provide technical knowledge, management and organizational skills, and access to

Table 6.1 Motivations of investors targeting developing countries

Type of motivation	Indications in %
Access to new sales markets	87
Lower costs of production factors	51
Coordination of the value chain	39
Purchasing a company with unique technology or valuable brand	15
Access to natural resources	12

Source: Own elaboration based on *GIC Survey 2017–2018*.

Table 6.2 The comparison of FDI investors' motivations in developed and developing countries

Motivations	Developed countries	Developing countries
Market size	Important	Very important
Natural resources	Not important	Very important
Qualified workforce	Very important	Not important
Cheap workforce	Not important	Very important
International brands	Important	Not important
Local brands	Not important	Important
Access to capital	Very important	Not important
Macroeconomic factors	Important	Important
Economic freedom	Important	Not important
Access to new technologies	Very important	Not important
Coordination of the value chain	Important	Important
Technological advancement of society	Important	Not important

Source: Own elaboration.

foreign markets. Moreover, FDI have significant potential to transform economies through innovation, increasing productivity and creating better paid and more stable jobs in the host countries, sectors that attract FDI and supporting industries (Arnold, Smarzynska Javorcik, & Mattoo, 2011; Bijsterbosch & Kolasa, 2009; Echandi, Krajcovicova, & Qiang, 2015; Rizvi & Nishat, 2009). Foreign investors slowly become increasingly important players in providing global public goods, combating climate change, improving working conditions, setting global industry standards and providing infrastructure to local communities.

Links between foreign companies and local partners or suppliers may promote the transfer of foreign companies' technologies, knowledge and practices, but also requirements that may help domestic suppliers improve their technical and quality standards (Du, Harrison, & Jefferson, 2011; Farole & Winkler, 2014; Smarzynska Javorcik & Spatareanu, 2009). A study conducted in Turkey suggests that interactions between MNEs and their Turkish suppliers facilitate the upgrading of local products (Smarzynska Javorcik, Lo Turco, & Maggioni, 2017). The analyses of the companies' activity in Lithuania and Vietnam show that there are positive side effects of productivity resulting from FDI through links between foreign subsidiaries and their local suppliers (Smarzynska Javorcik, 2004; Newman, Rand, Talbot, & Tarp, 2015).

FDIs in the UK

The first FDIs of European companies in the UK took place already in the second half of the nineteenth century (Young, Hood, & Dunlop, 1988). Figure 6.2 presents a comparison of the largest European economies (the UK, Germany,

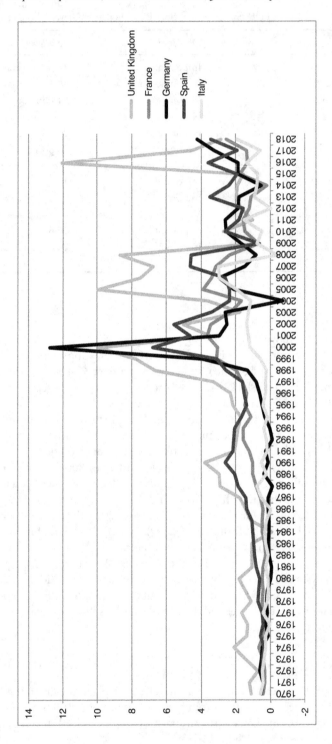

Figure 6.2 The net value of incoming FDIs (in % of GDP) of the largest European economies, in 1970–2017

Source: Own elaboration based on UNCTAD (2020).

France, Italy and Spain) in terms of the net value of inflows FDI expressed as a percentage of GDP in the years 1970–2017. Over the period of 48 years, the net value of FDI inflows to the UK in in relative terms was the highest among the analyzed countries in 32 cases. At the same time, during the remaining 16 years, only three times has the indicator for the UK been lower than for all the other countries. This situation occurred in 1984, 2009 and 2011. In addition, for the remaining 13 years as many as six times (1991, 2000, 2002, 2010 and 2013–2014), the net value of incoming FDI obtained by the UK was the second highest value among the compared economies.

Considering the nominal net value of incoming FDI (expressed in current USD prices) in the years 1970–2017, the UK attracted a higher value of investments than Spain – except for 1984 and 2011 – and Italy, except for 1984, 2009 and 2011. In the analyzed period, the value of FDI attracted by France was higher than the value obtained by the UK only in 1984, 1992–1995, 2003, 2009 and 2011. In the aggregate, the net value of FDI attracted by the UK in 1970–2017 was more than twice as high as the value obtained by France (2.20), almost twice as high as Germany (1.82), more than three times as high as Spain (3.08) and more than five times as high as Italy (5.66).

The role of companies holding foreign capital in the UK economy is evident when considering their share in the number of companies operating in the UK, but also in the turnover and employment they generate. According to the data from March 2017, there were 28,835 foreign capital companies operating in the UK (Office for National Statistics, 2018). Of these, 41.37% were owned by foreign shareholders from the EU. Companies with foreign participation constituted only 1.08% of all enterprises operating in the UK. At the same time, companies with foreign capital accounted for 14.44% of employment and 36.30% of turnover generated in the UK business sector. While a company with foreign participation employed on average about 152 employees, companies with local capital employed about 10 people. An even greater difference exists in terms of generated turnover. In March 2017, an average annual turnover of foreign equity companies operating in the UK amounted to approximately GBP 65.4 million. During the same period, companies with local capital on average generated a turnover of approximately GBP 1.3 million. The results of conducted empirical research also indicate that in 1992–1996 in the UK, the productivity of foreign subsidiaries of multinational companies was higher than that of local companies, and that foreign subsidiaries employed higher levels of human capital and benefited from higher economies of scale (Wang, Siler, & Liu, 2002).

The long presence of companies with foreign capital in the UK and the important role they play in the UK economy have attracted the interest of numerous researchers of international companies (e.g., Birkinshaw, Hood, & Young, 2005; Dimitratos, Liouka, & Young, 2014; Hood, Young, & La, 1994; Kottaridi, Filippaios, Papanastassiou, & Pearce, 2004; McDonald, Tüselmann, Voronkova, & Dimitratos, 2005; Papanastassiou & Pearce, 1997; Pearce & Papanastassiou, 1996; Qu, 2007; Taggart, 1996; Williams, 2003; Young, Hood, &

Hamill, 1988). From the perspective of Brexit's influence on the international-ization and competitiveness of Polish companies, what is particularly interesting is the research focused on the roles of subsidiaries located in the UK and their evolution. In the context of hard Brexit, this research is valuable as parts of it concern changes in tariff conditions for foreign subsidiaries operating in the UK in the context of the EEA development. The remaining section of this subchapter focuses on discussing the results of the research related to this issue.

Papanastassiou and Pearce (1998) conducted multiple studies on aspects related to the positioning of R&D activities of 190 subsidiaries of multinational companies located in the UK and operating within the manufacturing industry in 1993–1994. On this basis, the authors define four types of roles as follows (Papanastassiou & Pearce, 1998):

- the production of products for the UK market that are available in the range of the international company;
- the production and export of a specified range of products of an interna-tional company in the European supply network;
- the production and export of parts and components (for assembly else-where) in the European supply network of an international company; and
- the development, production and sales of products for the UK or European market (or broader), which are new to the existing product portfolio of an international company.

Regarding the first role, Pearce and Papanastassiou (1996) emphasize that increasing globalization and competition causes this type of subsidiaries' roles to become increasingly rare, even though in 1993–1994 it still accounted for a significant share of foreign subsidiaries of international companies. In terms of R&D functions, the subsidiaries performing this kind of role are strongly dependent on multinational companies and focus their activities on using stan-dardized technologies – created and used in an international company – to adapt them to local markets.

The second role involves the production and export of a specific range of products to a wider European market. This role is still determined by a centrally coordinated network of an international company, simultaneously subordinated to the satisfaction of needs beyond the national territory. Therefore, unlike the first role, here the localization of R&D function in the UK does not entail the benefits of proximity to the target market. As a result, according to Papanas-tassiou and Pearce (1998), the probability of fulfilling the R&D function in the second role is lower. However, if this function is assigned to a subsidiary company performing this type of role, it will be of greater importance within an international company and simultaneously subordinate to the achievement of a given region's objectives.

As for the third role, Papanastassiou and Pearce (1998) indicate that it was already relatively rare in the 1990s for foreign subsidiaries of multinational com-panies located in the UK. One of the reasons for this is the importance of cost motives in choosing the location of such companies. Furthermore, Papanastas-siou and Pearce (1998) note that these companies perform the R&D function relatively rarely.

In the fourth role, the probability of performing R&D functions is the highest. Moreover, this function is to play a central role in relation to the proactive activities of such a unit within the international company. At the same time, R&D activities should be part of the overall product policy of the multinational company, exploit existing dependencies and create synergies.

In the case of hard Brexit, UK-based foreign subsidiaries of multinational companies that perform roles other than the production of products available in the range of the multinational company for the UK market are at a relative disadvantage compared to sister companies located in member states of the EEA. As mentioned earlier, this is even more important because, in 2017, 41.37% of all foreign subsidiaries located in the UK originated from the EU (Office for National Statistics, 2018). In view of the free movement of goods and services in the EEA, the likelihood that most of these subsidiaries were solely tasked with manufacturing products and providing services to the UK market seems quite low. Moreover, it is highly likely that a significant number of foreign subsidiaries with owners from outside the EU also performed responsibilities beyond the UK and were motivated by access to the common European market. Hood et al. (1994) – whose study focused on a representative sample of 16 subsidiaries of Japanese corporations located in Scotland – also indicate the dominance of this trend, according to whom about 56% of the analyzed companies were engaged in serving the wider European market. These companies showed significant trade relations with sister companies located in Europe, in terms of both product reception and the supply of intermediates and raw materials.

Moreover, studies of Taggart (1996) on the sample of 123 Scotland-based subsidiaries of international companies operating in the manufacturing sector, so as to indicate that a significant expansion of markets served by the subsidiaries occurred already in 1989–1994. In particular, the scope of duties performed in the analyzed companies was extended from the home area to the European area. Furthermore, this trend was to be continued in 1994–1999 (Taggart, 1996). Taggart (1996) also indicate the important role of foreign subsidiaries in the development of the host country's economy through external embeddedness. In the context of Brexit, the consequences of the external embeddedness of subsidiaries located in the UK are equally important. On the one hand, links with local companies may help to reduce customs charges. On the other hand, should the market scope of foreign subsidiaries be limited, local suppliers are also threatened with a reduction in their scale of operations. Therefore, the UK's withdrawal from the EU also threatens to worsen the competitiveness of foreign subsidiaries located in the UK against entities operating within the EEA. Moreover, the results of empirical research show that the location of a foreign subsidiary in Europe – but in a country outside the EU – is less attractive for international companies in terms of the number of value chain functions they perform and their level of competence.

At the end of 2012, the state of receivables of Polish FDI in the UK amounted to EUR 4,306.8 million and indicated the UK as the third largest Polish investment location abroad (after Luxembourg and Cyprus; Kazimierczak, 2015). Expansion into the UK market through FDI was conducted by such companies as Fakro, Nowy Styl, Inglot, LPP, Can-Pack, Wielton, Press Glass, Elemental Holding, Rec Global, Comarch, Black Red White, Forte, Amika, Tele-fonika Kable and Rawlplug (Błaszczak, 2017; Kazimierczak, 2015; Puls Biznesu, 2018).

The UK attractiveness for FDI in the context of Brexit and the COVID-19 pandemic

The above findings about the causes of FDI in developed countries – i.e., the development of technologies supporting sustainable development – are mostly confirmed in the case of the UK. The main advantage of the British economy, significant for attracting FDI, is its strong liberal character in comparison to other European economies. Therefore, the British business environment is exceptionally favorable to foreign investors. The UK economy is ranked eighth in the World Bank's *Doing Business 2020* ranking, which is one position higher than in the previous year. In the classification of *Global Competitiveness Report 2019*, the UK ranks in the ninth position, which is one position lower than the previous year.

Still, the UK is a very attractive country for investors. In *Doing Business 2020*, the UK surpasses all large developed countries in terms of the ease in starting a new business, ranking eighth. For comparison, the United States ranked 55th, Germany – 125th and France – 37th. In terms of investor protection, the UK ranks seventh, while the United States – 36th, Germany – 61st and France – 45th.

When analyzing the number of investment projects implemented in the UK in 2019, the largest number of investments came from the United States – 375 projects, Germany – 50 projects, France – 37, Canada and Australia 36, respectively. The increasing American investment only stresses the UK's attractiveness especially in the high-tech industries. The UK is the leader of European countries in attracting the number of direct foreign investments in the know-how area.

The liberal economic policy of successive governments has always sought to create a stable but flexible and attractive economic environment for FDI. Foreign companies are treated in the UK like British companies. The British government is a strong advocate of equal rights for all companies operating in the UK regardless of the nationality of capital.

In the first quarter of 2020, the consulting company EY conducted a survey among more than 500 boards of various European companies on the attractiveness of the UK as a location for FDI in the context of Brexit and the COVID-19 pandemic (EY, 2020). We may learn from EY survey what factors influence investors' decisions regarding the choice of country when deciding on FDI, in this case those located in the UK (Table 6.3).

Table 6.3 Main factors influencing investors' decisions on the location of FDI in the UK

Factors	Indications in %
Liquidity of financial markets and availability of capital	30
Staff qualifications	25
Quality of necessary government support	23
Success in combating the COVID-19 pandemic	23
Country competitiveness in terms of costs	23
Reliability of national infrastructure (transportation, telecommunication and energy)	22
Level of new technologies adaptation by customers, citizens and administration	22
Availability of (skilled and unskilled) workforce	21
Stability of political and regulatory institutions	20
Safety and security measures taken to prevent crises (health, environment and internet)	20
Strength of the national market	19
Quality of life and cultural diversity	19
Weight of national stimulus packages for business	18
Government approach to climate change	18

Source: Own elaboration based on EY (2020).

When analyzing the results of the research, it is worth noting a slight discrepancy that divides the individual criteria determining the choice of destination in which the company would invest. So far, the most important factors were the expert knowledge and the available infrastructure, but as a result of the pandemic, the number of criteria considered has expanded. Recently, the British government stresses the importance of the climate change and the increasing geographical disparities. The emergence of the COVID-19 pandemic has accelerated the shift of government priorities as it now focuses on the balance between economic growth, the environment and lifestyle. Investors highlight the availability of private finance in the UK, and the role that the government can play in the economy by both responding to COVID-19 and providing additional funding. Both issues seem to be priorities for investors considering starting a business in the UK.

The EY study also forecasts the importance of various industries in the near future (Table 6.4). Cleantech and renewables industry (39%) as well as digital economy (35%) occupy the top of the ranking. The cleantech industry deals with the broadly understood support of environmental protection, renewable energy.

Cleantech – or the clean technology industry – includes processes, products and services that reduce the negative impact on the environment through significant improvements in energy efficiency, sustainable use of resources or environmental protection measures. Among others, cleantech includes industries related to recycling, renewable energy, information technology, green transport, electric motors, hydrogen technology, green chemistry, lighting and gray water. Cleantech products and services improve operational efficiency while reducing costs, energy consumption, waste or environmental pollution. This is the result of the increased interest of consumers, regulators and industry in environmentally neutral forms of energy generation.

In connection with the above issues, entrepreneurs were also asked about the anticipated trends resulting from the COVID-19 pandemic in the next three years (Table 6.5). By far the most frequently indicated answers were automation processes that will replace people (81% of indications), emphasis on sustainable development and climate protection (61%), and the reversal of globalization processes (57%).

In the EY survey, the respondents were asked about the main threats affecting the attractiveness of Europe as an FDI location in the coming years. The results

Table 6.4 Mentions of sectors that will drive development in the coming years

Industry	Indications in %
Cleantech and renewables	39
Digital economy	35
Healthcare and wellbeing	24
Energy and utilities	20
Consumer industry	16
Mobility	15
Bank, finance and insurance	13
Professional services	12
Real estate and construction	10

Source: Own elaboration based on (EY, 2020).

Table 6.5 Developmental trends anticipated after the COVID-19 pandemic

	Indications in %
Implementing technologies that will replace people	81
Focusing on environmental protection and combating climate change	61
Reversal of globalization processes	57
Digitization of customer access to services	52
Government interventions in economic regulation	25
Reducing supply chains to Europe	20
Geopolitical tensions	4

Source: own elaboration based on EY (2020).

Table 6.6 Most important threats to the attractiveness of Europe as an FDI recipient

Types of threats to the attractiveness of Europe	2020	2019
Brexit	24%	38%
Political instability of the EU	21%	35%
Aging of the population	21%	20%
Climate change	19%	–
Increased populist/protectionist attitudes	19%	22%
Global and regional geopolitical instability	18%	21%
Migration flows	16%	13%
Tax and economic policy reform in the United States	16%	20%
Competition from developing markets	16%	17%
Sharp decline in growth in China	15%	15%
Tax system (amount and complexity of taxes)	15%	–
Uncertainty regarding tariffs and trade policy/ slowdown in global trade flows	14%	15%
Lack of qualified workers	13%	14%
Europe's limited innovation capacity	10%	9%
Lack of funding	6%	7%
High volatility of foreign exchange, commodity and capital markets	6%	10%
Other factors	4%	2%

Source: own elaboration based on EY (2020).

are presented in Table 6.6. Brexit turned out to be the biggest threat (24% of indications), although its significance has decreased in relation to 2019 (38%), when a similar survey was conducted.

The results of the EY survey indicate that investors' intentions toward the UK, compared to other FDI destinations in Europe, remain relatively positive (Table 6.7). The respondents' answers reveal that 65% of the projects planned in the UK continue; 6% of the investors even increased their investments in the light of COVID-19. Only 3% say they cancelled their plans completely. On the other hand, analogical data regarding Europe reveal a more cautious approach of investors, with 66% planning to cut investments and 23% withholding them, compared to 17% and 15% for the UK, respectively.

The view that the attractiveness of the UK for FDI is less exposed to the shock of COVID-19 than the rest of Europe is confirmed by other responses to the EY survey. When asked whether the UK and Europe will be more or less attractive for FDI within three years after the COVID-19 pandemic, investors answered negatively for both regions but relatively less negatively in relation to the UK's prospects (Table 6.8). The recovery from COVID-19 will be difficult, but there are some reasons for optimism in the investors' perception of the UK.

The UK left the EU on January 31, 2020, and the transition period is expected to end on December 31, 2020. The EY interviewers asked entrepreneurs

Table 6.7 Change in investment plans due to the COVID-19 pandemic

	UK	Europe
Planned investments were cancelled	3%	0%
Significant decrease in investment plans (more than 20%)	12%	15%
Small decrease in investment plans (less than 20%)	5%	51%
Periodic suspension of planned investments	15%	23%
No changes in planned investments	59%	11%
Increase in planned investments	6%	0%

Source: Own elaboration based on EY (2020).

Table 6.8 Change in the attractiveness of the UK and Europe after the COVID-19 pandemic

	UK	Europe
Significant increase in attractiveness	6%	0%
Slight increase in attractiveness	28%	9%
No changes	12%	26%
Slight decline in attractiveness	34%	55%
Significant decrease in attractiveness	20%	9%

Source: Own elaboration based on EY (2020).

Table 6.9 Assessment of attractiveness of the UK as a place for FDIs after Brexit

Change value	Indications in %
Significant increase in attractiveness	4
Slight increase in attractiveness	30
No changes	13
Slight decrease in attractiveness	42
Significant decrease in attractiveness	11

Source: Own elaboration based on EY (2020).

whether the future status of the UK outside the EU – with the possibility of pursuing independent policies of responding to future shocks – will make the country more or less attractive as the location for FDI. It turned out that that a slight majority (53%) expects a decrease in attractiveness, although only 11% believe it will be significant. Meanwhile, 34% expect an increase in attractiveness with a significantly positive change expected by 4% of the respondents (Table 6.9).

Conclusions

FDI is the most advanced form of internationalization of national economies. Its characteristic feature is a long-term relationship with the host country and, therefore, an impact on its economic and social processes. Over the last three decades, the value of annual FDI flows in the global scale increased 7.5 times, including 4.7 times for developed countries and almost 20 times for developing countries. The reasons for investing in developed and developing countries differ significantly.

The modern economic strategy of developed European countries – thus also the UK – is based on four great challenges of civilization: renewable energy sources, mobility, large data collections (Big Data) and the aging of populations. The investor survey conducted by EY in May 2020 identifies the trends and opportunities that will shape the UK economy in the future. The UK's technological power provides an opportunity to transform its economy; hence, new strategy should seek to maximize its potential for the development of digital technologies that can be implemented across the economy, especially if they can support the development of clean technologies, health and social well-being. Together with digital technology, these sectors should form the core of a new industrial strategy, which should also be developed from the bottom up, with the involvement of local governments. Such an approach will ensure that the UK may continue to be an attractive place for FDIs.

References

Alam, A., & Zulfiqar Ali Shah, S. (2013). Determinants of foreign direct investment in OECD member countries. *Journal of Economic Studies*, *40*(4), 515–527. https://doi.org/10.1108/JES-10-2011-0132

Apergis, N., Economidou, C., & Filippidis, I. (2008). Innovation technology transfer and labor productivity linkages: Evidence from a panel of manufacturing industries. *Review of World Economics*, *144*(3), 491–508. https://doi.org/10.1007/s10290-008-0157-9

Arnold, J., Smarzynska Javorcik, B. S., & Mattoo, A. (2011). Does services liberalization benefit manufacturing firms? Evidence from the Czech Republic. *Journal of International Economics*, *85*(1), 136–146. https://doi.org/10.1016/j.jinteco.2011.05.002

Asiedu, E. (2006). Foreign direct investment in Africa: The role of natural resources, market size, government policy, institutions and political instability. *The World Economy*, *29*(1), 63–77. https://doi.org/10.2139/ssrn.717361

Asiedu, E., & Lien, D. (2004). Capital controls and foreign direct investment. *World Development*, *32*(3), 479–490. https://doi.org/10.1016/j.worlddev.2003.06.016

Azam, M., & Lukman, L. (2010). Determinants of foreign direct investment in India, Indonesia and Pakistan: A quantitative approach. *Journal of Managerial Sciences*, *4*(1), 31–43. Retrieved from www.qurtuba.edu.pk/jms/default_files/JMS/4_1/02_azam.pdf

Bevan, A., Estrin, S., & Meyer, K. (2004). Foreign investment location and institutional development in transition economies. *International Business Review*, *13*(1), 43–64. https://doi.org/10.1016/j.ibusrev.2003.05.005

Bijsterbosch, M., & Kolasa, M. (2009). *FDI and productivity convergence in central and Eastern Europe: An industry-level investigation*. Frankfurt: European Central Bank.

Birkinshaw, J., Hood, N., & Young, S. (2005). Subsidiary entrepreneurship, internal and external competitive forces, and subsidiary performance. *International Business Review*, *14*(2), 227–248. https://doi.org/10.1016/j.ibusrev.2004.04.010

Błaszczak, A. (2017). Desant polskich firm na Wyspy Brytyjskie (Polish companies charging the British market). *Rzeczpospolita*. Retrieved December 31, 2017 from www.rp.pl/Biznes/310309875-Desant-polskich-firm-na-Wyspy-Brytyjskie.html

Chang, C. C., & Luh, Y.-H. (2000). Efficiency change and the growth in productivity: The Asian growth experience. *Journal of Asian Economics*, *10*(4), 551–570. https://doi.org/10.1016/S1049-0078(00)00032-4

Dimitratos, P., Liouka, I., & Young, S. (2014). A missing operationalization: Entrepreneurial competencies in multinational enterprise subsidiaries. *Long Range Planning*, *47*(1–2), 64–75. https://doi.org/10.1016/j.lrp.2013.10.004

Du, L., Harrison, A., & Jefferson, G. (2011). *Do institutions matter for FDI spillovers? The implications of China's 'special characteristics'*. Cambridge: National Bureau of Economic Research.

Dunning, J. H., & Lundan, S. M. (2008). *Multinational enterprises and the global economy*. Cheltenham: Edward Elgar Publishing.

Echandi, R., Krajcovicova, J., & Qiang, C. Z. W. (2015). *The impact of investment policy in a changing global economy: A review of the literature*. Washington, DC: World Bank Group.

EY. (2020). *Attractiveness survey UK*. Retrieved from https://assets.ey.com/content/dam/ey-sites/ey-com/en_uk/topics/attractiveness/ey-uk-attractiveness-survey-may2020.pdf

Farole, T., & Winkler, D. (2014). *Making foreign direct investment work for sub-Saharan Africa: Local spillovers and competitiveness in global value Chains*. Washington, DC: World Bank Group.

Greene, J., & Villanueva, D. (1991). Private investment in developing countries: An empirical analysis. *IMF Staff Papers*, *38*(1), 33–58. Retrieved from www.elibrary.imf.org/view/IMF024/14681-9781451956917/14681-9781451956917/14681-9781451956917_A002.xml?language=en&redirect=true

Henisz, W., & Swaminathan, A. (2008). Introduction: Institutions and international business. *Journal of International Business Studies*, *39*(4), 537–539. https://doi.org/10.1057/palgrave.jibs

Hood, N., Young, S., & La, D. (1994). Strategic evolution within Japanese manufacturing plants in Europe: UK evidence. *International Business Review*, *3*(2), 97–122. https://doi.org/10.1016/0969-5931(94)90018-3

Kazimierczak, D. (2015). *Kto i gdzie inwestuje (Who invests where?)*. Retrieved June 17, 2017 from https://uk.trade.gov.pl/pl/wielka-brytania/inwestycje/1667,kto-i-gdzie-inwestuje.html

Kok, R., & Acikgoz Ersoy, B. (2009). Analyses of FDI determinants in developing countries. *International Journal of Social Economics*, *36*(1/2), 105–123. https://doi.org/10.1108/03068290910921226

Kottaridi, C., Filippaios, F., Papanastassiou, M., & Pearce, R. (2004). Choice of location and the roles of foreign subsidiaries: Evidence from UK regions. *Henley Business School Working Papers*. Reading.

Leitão, N. C., & Faustino, H. C. (2010). Determinants of foreign direct investment in Portugal. *The Journal of Applied Business and Economics*, *11*(3), 19–26.

Levin, R. (2001). International financial liberalization and economic growth. *Review of International Economics*, *9*(4), 688–702. https://doi.org/10.1111/1467-9396.00307

Li, X., & Liu, X. (2005). Foreign direct investment and economic growth: An increasingly endogenous relationship. *World Development*, *33*(3), 393–407. https://doi.org/10.1016/j.worlddev.2004.11.001

Masuku, M. B., & Dlamini, T. S. (2009). Determinants of foreign direct investment inflows in Swaziland. *Journal of Development and Agricultural Economics*, *1*(5), 177–184. Retrieved from https://www.researchgate.net/publication/228763573_Determinants_of_foreign_direct_investment_inflows_in_Swaziland

McDonald, F., Tüselmann, H.-J., Voronkova, S., & Dimitratos, P. (2005). The strategic development of foreign-owned subsidiaries and direct employment in host locations in the United Kingdom. *Environment and Planning C: Politics and Space*, *23*(6), 867–882. https://doi.org/10.1068/c0443

Mina, W. (2009). External commitment mechanisms, institutions, and FDI in GCC countries. *Journal of International Financial Markets, Institutions and Money, 19*(2), 371–386. https://doi.org/10.1016/j.intfin.2008.02.001

Miskinis, A., & Juozenaite, I. (2015). A comparative analysis of foreign direct investment factors. *Ekonomika, 94*(2), 7–27. https://doi.org/10.15388/Ekon.2015.2.8230

Newman, C., Rand, J., Talbot, T., & Tarp, F. (2015). Technology transfers, foreign investment and productivity spillovers. *European Economic Review, 76*, 168–187. https://doi.org/10.1016/j.euroecorev.2015.02.005

Office for National Statistics. (2018). *Analysis of foreign ownership by region 2018*. London: Office for National Statistics. Retrieved from www.ons.gov.uk/economy/nationalaccounts/balanceofpayments/articles/ukforeigndirectinvestmenttrendsandanalysis/july2018

Papanastassiou, M., & Pearce, R. D. (1997). Technology sourcing and the strategic roles of manufacturing subsidiaries in the UK: Local competences and global competitiveness. *Management International Review, 37*(1), 5–25. Retrieved from www.jstor.org/stable/40228385

Papanastassiou, M., & Pearce, R. D. (1998). Individualism and interdependence in the technological development of MNEs: The strategic positioning of R&D in overseas subsidiaries. In J. Birkinshaw & N. Hood (Eds.), *Multinational corporate evolution and subsidiary development* (pp. 50–75). Houndmills: Macmillan.

Pearce, R. D., & Papanastassiou, M. (1996). R&D networks and innovation: De-centralised product development in multinational enterprises. *R&D Management, 26*(4), 315–333. https://doi.org/10.1111/j.1467-9310.1996.tb00968.x

Piteli, E. E. N. (2010). Determinants of foreign direct investment in developed economies: A comparison between European and non-European countries. *Contributions to Political Economy, 29*(1), 111–128. https://doi.org/10.1093/cpe/bzq004

Puls Biznesu. (2018). *Wielka Brytania przyciąga polskie przedsiębiorstwa (The UK attracts Polish FDI)*. Retrieved from www.pb.pl/wielka-brytania-przyciaga-polskie-przedsiebiorstwa-948282

Qu, R. (2007). The role of market orientation in the business success of MNCs' UK subsidiaries. *Management Decision, 45*(7), 1181–1192. https://doi.org/10.1108/00251740710773970

Rizvi, S. Z. A., & Nishat, M. (2009). The impact of foreign direct investment on employment opportunities: Panel data analysis: Empirical evidence from Pakistan, India and China. *The Pakistan Development Review, 48*(4), 841–851. https://doi.org/10.30541/v48i4IIpp.841-851

Saini, N., & Singhania, M. (2018). Determinants of FDI in developed and developing countries: A quantitative analysis using GMM. *Journal of Economic Studies, 45*(2), 348–382. https://doi.org/10.1108/JES-07-2016-0138

Singhania, M., & Gupta, A. (2011). Determinants of foreign direct investment in India. *Journal of International Trade Law and Policy, 10*(1), 64–82. https://doi.org/10.1108/14770021111116142

Smarzynska Javorcik, B. (2004). Does FDI increase the productivity of domestic firms? In search of spillovers through backward linkages. *American Economic Review, 94*(3), 605–627. https://doi.org/10.1257/0002828041464605

Smarzynska Javorcik, B., Lo Turco, A., & Maggioni, D. (2017). New and improved: Does FDI boost production complexity in host countries? *The Economic Journal, 128*(614), 2507–2537. https://doi.org/10.1111/ecoj.12530

Smarzynska Javorcik, B., & Spatareanu, M. (2009). Tough love: Do Czech suppliers learn from their relationships with multinationals? *Scandinavian Journal of Economics, 111*(4), 811–833. https://doi.org/10.1111/j.1467-9442.2009.01591.x

Taggart, J. H. (1996). Multinational manufacturing subsidiaries in Scotland: Strategic role and economic impact. *International Business Review, 5*(5), 447–468. https://doi.org/10.1080/00343408812331345160

UNCTAD. (2020). *World investment report*. Retrieved from https://unctad.org/en/Pages/DIAE/World%20Investment%20Report/Annex-Tables.aspx

Wang, Ch., Siler, P., & Liu, X. (2002). The relative economic performance of foreign subsidiaries in UK manufacturing. *Applied Economics*, *34*(15), 1885–1892. https://doi.org/10.1080/00036840210128762

Wiktor, J. W. (2005). *Rynek Unii Europejskiej. Koncepcja i zasady funkcjonowania (European Union market: Concept and principles of functioning)*. Cracow: Wydawnictwo Akademii Ekonomicznej w Krakowie.

Williams, D. (2003). Explaining employment changes in foreign manufacturing investment in the UK. *International Business Review*, *12*(4), 479–497. https://doi.org/10.1016/S0969-5931(03)00040-4

Woo, J. (2009). Productivity growth and technological diffusion through foreign direct investment. *Economic Inquiry*, *47*(2), 226–248. https://doi.org/10.1111/j.1465-7295.2008.00166.x

World Bank. (2018). *Global investment competitiveness report 2017/2018*. Washington, DC: World Bank Group. Retrieved from https://openknowledge.worldbank.org/handle/10986/28493

Xiaming, L., Parker, D., Kirit, V., & Yingqi, W. (2001). The impact of foreign direct investment on labour productivity in the Chinese electronics industry. *International Business Review*, *10*(4), 421–439. https://doi.org/10.1016/S0969-5931(01)00024-5

Young, S., Hood, N., & Dunlop, S. (1988). Global strategies, multinational subsidiary roles and economic impact in Scotland. *Regional Studies*, *22*(6), 487–497. https://doi.org/10.1080/00343408812331345160

Young, S., Hood, N., & Hamill, J. (1988). *Foreign multinationals and the British economy*. London: Routledge.

Zhang, Z. (2002). Productivity and economic growth: An empirical assessment of the contribution of FDI to the Chinese economy. *Journal of Economic Development*, *27*(2), 81–94. Retrieved from https://ideas.repec.org/a/jed/journl/v27y2002i2p81-94.html

7 What drives companies' strategies in the face of Brexit?

Cezary Główka, Marian Gorynia, Aleksandra Kania, Katarzyna Mroczek-Dąbrowska

Introduction

The UK's membership in the EU guaranteed Polish enterprises free access to the British market on terms set out in the Treaty on EU and the Treaty on the Functioning of the EU. British citizens' decision of June 2016 caused concern among entrepreneurs about the free movement of goods, services, capital and employees to and from the UK. The actual Brexit happened only on January 31, 2020. For over three and a half years, the British government and the European Commission have been engaged in difficult negotiations on future relations. For Polish enterprises dealing in the British market, the most important issue is access to this market, i.e., the UK's economic relations with the EU. We still don't know what the relationship will be, because the European treaties did not provide any roadmap for the departure of a member state from the community.

Negotiations on the UK's access to the Common Market continue, and the concerns of companies remain unappeased. Due to the lack of agreement between the parties, enterprises bear high risk in strategic decisions. Development strategies, especially strategies for entering the British market and expansion or limiting company presence on this market, are burdened with the lack of knowledge about the outcome of the negotiations and the final shape of the UK-EU relations. On the other hand, enterprises economically connected with the UK cannot count on retaining their status quo. Following the decision of British citizens to withdraw from the EU, company strategies on the British market had to be adjusted. Therefore, it is interesting to investigate which companies – and based on which factors – made these adjustments in the negotiations period. Research results could enable us to better understand enterprises' decisions. Which forms of presence on the British market were preferred by Polish companies? Which industries were ready to take the risk of development, and which were waiting for the negotiations to be completed? Has the British market remained an attractive destination for companies already present on this market or have the companies decided to transfer their international activity to markets of other member states? How important are political factors for companies? Are the political factors as important as strictly economic factors like market, cost and competitiveness? Moreover, we will seek answers whether the companies secured themselves in advance. Has Brexit influenced the strategies of companies with foreign capital – especially with British capital – rather than companies with exclusively Polish capital? Finally, how has Brexit influenced the strategies of businesses of all sizes?

Empirical study on factors that determine company's operations in the British market

According to the British–Polish Chamber of Commerce, there are about 40,000 Polish companies active in the British market. In order to ensure accurate results, companies had to fulfill the following criteria to be included in the sample:

- employ at least 10 employees and generate net revenue of minimum PLN 2 million;
- prove financial stability through at least three years prior to the study;
- have been engaged in trade relations with the UK for at least six years prior to the study;
- their involvement in the British market had to remain a vital aspect to the company's functioning, e.g., by creating an important share in the company's revenue, being the target market for key products/services of the firm, hosting strategic clients for the company; and
- function in both production and non-production industries.

Since Statistics Poland does not provide a clear record of companies trading or investing in the UK with a division by industry (Nace Rev. 2 Codes), size and entry mode, the companies selected for the sample reflected the overall characteristics of Polish companies exporting their goods and services.

The study was conducted with the use of computer-assisted telephone interviews (CATIs) on a sample of $N = 500$ enterprises that operated on the British market. The respondents were representatives of management boards and heads of departments responsible for foreign affairs. The overwhelming majority of companies participating in the study did not have foreign capital (349 companies), and British capital was involved in only 12 companies (Table 7.1).

Table 7.1 Number of companies with foreign/British capital

Number of companies	Share of foreign capital
356	0%–20%
32	21%–40%
27	41%–60%
12	61%–80%
73	81%–100%

Source: Own elaboration.

Most of the companies participating in the study were not part of any capital groups, belonged to different size categories, achieved various revenues and operated in different industries (Tables 7.2–7.5).

The research included companies which level of internationalization was also varied, but those that were present on at least two foreign markets in 2017–2019. Table 7.6 shows their international activity.

Among the three most important markets, the largest numbers were mentioned from the UK (395 responses), Germany (376 responses) and Russia (102 responses). The average share of transactions performed on foreign markets in relation to total transactions in 2017–2019 and the involvement of teams in servicing foreign markets are shown in the Table 7.7 along with the dominant entry modes (Table 7.8).

Table 7.2 Number of companies that were part of an international/Polish capital group

Number of companies	Participation in an international capital group
409	No
91	Yes
Number of companies	Participation in a Polish capital group
425	No
75	Yes

Source: Own elaboration.

Table 7.3 Approximate number of full-time employees in years 2017–2019

Number of full-time employees	Number of companies
From 10 up to 49 employees	270
From 50 up to 249 employees	55
Above 250 employees	175

Source: Own elaboration.

Table 7.4 Average annual revenues of companies from the basic activity (in years 2017–2019)

Number of companies	Annual revenues
Up to PLN 10,000,000	118
From PLN 10,000,001 up to PLN 100,000,000	277
From PLN 100,000,001 up to PLN 999,000,000	105

Source: Own elaboration.

Table 7.5 The main activity of the company according to the PKD 2007 code classification

Number of companies	Section	PKD 2007 code classification
30	A	01 Crop and animal production, hunting and related service activities
8	A	03 Fishing and aquaculture
Total A – 38		AGRICULTURE, FORESTRY AND FISHING
4	B	07 Mining of metal ores
8	B	08 Other mining and quarrying
Total B – 12		MINING AND QUARRYING
34	C	10 Manufacture of food products
12	C	13 Manufacture of textiles
5	C	14 Manufacture of wearing apparel
8	C	15 Manufacture of leather and related products
6	C	17 Manufacture of paper and paper products
7	C	18 Printing and reproduction of recorded media
11	C	20 Manufacture of chemicals and chemical products
3	C	21 Manufacture of basic pharmaceutical products and pharmaceutical
27	C	22 Manufacture of rubber and plastic products
9	C	23 Manufacture of other non-metallic mineral products
8	C	24 Manufacture of basic metals
27	C	25 Manufacture of fabricated metal products, except machinery and equipment
10	C	26 Manufacture of computer, electronic and optical products
15	C	27 Manufacture of electrical equipment
21	C	28 Manufacture of machinery and equipment n.e.c.
16	C	29 Manufacture of motor vehicles, trailers and semi-trailers
3	C	30 Manufacture of other transport equipment
21	C	31 Manufacture of furniture
6	C	32 Other manufacturing
1	C	33 Repair and installation of machinery and equipment
Total C –250		MANUFACTURING
1	E	36 Water collection, treatment and supply
4	E	38 Waste collection, treatment and disposal activities; materials recovery
Total E – 5		WATER SUPPLY; SEWERAGE, WASTE MANAGEMENT AND REMEDIATION ACTIVITIES
1	F	41 Construction of buildings
1	F	42 Civil engineering
Total F – 2		CONSTRUCTION
16	G	45 Wholesale and retail trade and repair of motor vehicles and motorcycles

Number of companies	Section	PKD 2007 code classification
104	G	46 Wholesale trade, except of motor vehicles and motorcycles
5	G	47 Retail trade, except of motor vehicles and motorcycles
Total G –125		WHOLESALE AND RETAIL TRADE; REPAIR OF MOTOR VEHICLES AND MOTORCYCLES
8	H	49 Land transport and transport via pipelines
3	H	52 Warehousing and support activities for transportation
1	H	53 Postal and courier activities
Total H – 12		TRANSPORTATION AND STORAGE
1	I	56 Accommodation
Total I – 1		ACCOMMODATION AND FOOD SERVICE ACTIVITIES
9	J	58 Publishing activities
1	J	61 Telecommunications
7	J	62 Computer programming, consultancy and related activities
Total J – 17		INFORMATION AND COMMUNICATION
1	K	64 Financial service activities, except insurance and pension funding
1	K	66 Activities auxiliary to financial services and insurance activities
Total K – 2		FINANCIAL AND INSURANCE ACTIVITIES
1	L	68 Real estate activities
Total L – 1		REAL ESTATE ACTIVITIES
2	M	70 Activities of head offices; management consultancy activities
3	M	71 Architectural and engineering activities; technical testing and analysis
7	M	74 Other professional, scientific and technical activities
Total M – 12		PROFESSIONAL, SCIENTIFIC AND TECHNICAL ACTIVITIES
10	N	77 Rental and leasing activities
5	N	82 Office administrative, office support and other business support activities
Total N – 15		ADMINISTRATIVE AND SUPPORT SERVICE ACTIVITIES
2	R	93 Sports activities and amusement and recreation activities
Total R – 2		ARTS, ENTERTAINMENT AND RECREATION
4	S	95 Repair of computers and personal and household goods
2	S	96 Other personal service activities
Total S – 6		OTHER SERVICE ACTIVITIES

Source: Own elaboration.

Table 7.6 Number of foreign markets where the surveyed companies were present and the areas of their activity

Number of foreign markets (countries) where they were present	Number of companies
2–10	305
10–19	141
20–40	54
Area of international activity	Number of companies
Central and Eastern Europe	385
Western Europe	496
North America	75
South America	5
Africa	12
Asia	47
Concentrated on 1 market	91
Concentrated on 2 markets	323
Concentrated on 3 markets	67
Concentrated on 4 markets	16
Concentrated on 5 markets	3

Source: Own elaboration.

Table 7.7 Average share of transactions performed on foreign markets in relation to total transactions in years 2017–2019 and involvement of teams in servicing foreign markets

Average share of sales revenues generated on foreign markets in total sales revenues in years 2017–2019	Number of companies
5%–35%	144
35%–65%	182
70%–100%	174
Average share of sales revenues generated on the British market in total sales revenues in years 2017–2019	Number of companies
1%–9%	209
10%–10%	231
25%–60%	60
Average estimated share of the value of imports in the value of the company's purchases (%) in years 2017–2019	Number of companies
0%	94
5%–45%	194
50%–95%	212
Average estimated share of the value of imports from British suppliers in the company's purchases value (%) in years 2017–2019	Number of companies

Average share of sales revenues generated on foreign markets in total sales revenues in years 2017–2019	Number of companies
0%	169
2%–15%	264
18%–35%	67
Share of employees serving any activity on the British market/related to this market in relation to the total number of employees (%)	Number of companies
1%–8%	472
10%–14%	19
15%–20%	9

Source: Own elaboration.

Table 7.8 Form of entry and expansion on the British market in years 2017–2019

Indirect exporting	295
Direct exporting	414
Licensing	19
Franchising	13
Turnkey contracts	3
Strategic alliance	10
Joint venture	77
Greenfield	23
Acquisition	2
Managerial contracts	2
Other	0

Source: Own elaboration.

Hypotheses development

The development and formulation of hypotheses resulted from the synthesis of different theoretical concepts and sub-disciplines. On the macroeconomic level, these are new institutionalism, the concept of disintegration, international trade theory, FDI theories, economic geography, new trade theory and new new trade theory. On the mesoeconomic level, these concepts are industrial economics and – on the microeconomic level – strategic management, new institutional economics, the behavioral theory of the firm (Cyert & March, 1992) and international business. Important theoretical background for the whole research and the process of formulating hypotheses lies in the decision-making process under bounded rationality (Radner, 1996; Simon, 1972) and behavioral economics applied to firms (Mullainathan & Thaler, 2000). Thus, our hypotheses development reflected the influence of the macro-, meso- and microeconomic factors on decisions of Polish companies (Figure 7.1).

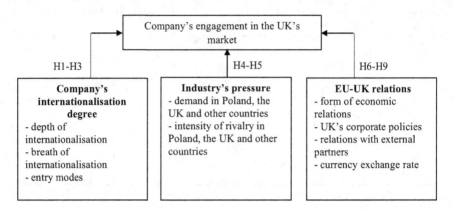

Figure 7.1 Research scheme

Source: Own elaboration.

The new institutional economics and transaction costs concepts especially explain some of the current questions on the internationalization process, including entry modes and the scale of foreign engagement (Williamson, 1985). The transaction cost theory divides the cost of fulfilling a contract into ex-ante and ex-post costs. The ex-ante transaction costs appear before conducting a transaction and include, among other things, market research, negotiation, safeguarding cost, contract preparation and opportunity prevention. Since many of those costs are not aligned with a singular transaction but bound with long-term relations, in the case of market abandonment companies would face a high level of sunken costs. Moreover, the quest to find an alternative market(s) or the need to scale down the production (or service) scope requires additional funds for either new investments or company's structure adaptation. Thus, we hypothesize that:

> H1: The stronger the companies' economic ties to the UK, the greater their engagement in that market regardless of the shape of the future UK–EU relations.

To draw further on the internationalization process, we should underline that the ex-ante costs differ significantly depending on the entry modes that companies undertake (Nicolaides & Roy, 2017). Companies that experience high transaction costs tend to favor equity over non-equity entry modes in order to maintain full control over their activities (Anderson & Gatignon, 1986; Brouthers, 2002). Countries like the UK – which have exhibited political stability over the years – have drawn numerous investments, including from Poland (NBP, 2016). In 2011–2016, the FDI position of Poland in the UK was stable in equity, investment fund shares and debt instruments (NBP, 2016). Since the Polish FDI in the British market brings stable and sufficient revenue flows and exiting the market would mean high disinvestment costs, we hypothesize that:

> H2: The companies that entered the UK with equity modes limit their engagement in the UK in a smaller degree compared to companies that entered with non-equity modes.

Furthermore, Sorensen (1997) suggests that internationalization concepts could be divided into four main groups that encompass: progressive models, contingency models, business networks and social constructions. These concepts shed different light on the internationalization process itself, but they all confirm that increasing the internationalization degree means for the company reaching more geographical locations (the breadth of internationalization), among other things. The Uppsala model argues that – with experience gained in time – companies are more likely to invest in more diversified locations. The "born-global" concept stresses that – due to highly competitive potential – companies are able and eager to undertake foreign expansion from the very beginning of their existence. One of the advantages of high geographical diversification is the mitigation of risk associated with operational functioning. The loss of revenue/profit experienced in one market can be compensated with the envisaged increase in another one. On the other hand, low geographical diversification implies higher dependence on a particular market, regardless of the changes that happen on this market. Therefore, we hypothesize that:

> H3: The higher the number of geographical locations the companies function in, the lower is their engagement in the UK.

One of the key motives to undertake international activities is market-seeking. One of its crucial assumptions is that a new destination is likely to generate enough growth to create future potential to develop and that the market is big enough to accommodate new ventures. The UK is ranked among the top ten economies in the world with the GDP of £1,940 trillion. Even with the decision to withdraw from the EU, the IMF estimates that by 2022 the UK's GDP will increase to £2,417 trillion. Growth estimations obviously depend on the industry and are interrelated with the parallel situation in other countries, thus we hypothesize that:

> H4: The higher the demand the companies experience in the UK and the lower the demand they experience in other countries, the greater their engagement in the UK.

Porter's (1980, 2008) Five Forces Framework enables us to determine the attractiveness of an industry. The framework considers the threat of new entrants, the existence of substitutes, the bargaining power of customers and suppliers and the level of industry rivalry. One of the factors that may drive companies to engage in foreign activities is the industry rivalry. Theories of industrial organization highlight that the industrial environment highly influences decisions made by companies. If companies function in an environment of high rivalry, they may be forced to compete for market shares. Moreover, if a market exhibits over-saturation and the industry is in a mature or decline stage, the pressure to seek other revenue sources grows. Similarly, some companies do not initiate foreign expansion but follow home competitors. They do it for different reasons, e.g., to bridge the competitive gap between them and their rivals, to gain new markets, to reduce their costs. Therefore, we hypothesize that:

> H5: The lower the rivalry the companies experience in the UK and the higher the rivalry they experience in other countries, the greater their engagement in the UK.

We should ask what the next step after the British voters' decision would be. One of the potential answers is a redefinition of the UK-EU relations. According to Article 50 of the Treaty of the EU, we might expect a negotiation process, arrangements for the withdrawal and a new relationship between the withdrawing country and the EU (Lazowski, 2012). According to Nicolaides (2013, p. 214), "the most extensive impact of exit (i.e., withdrawing from the EU) is likely to be ending of the right of access to the Internal Market". The Internal Market can be defined as a market without internal barriers (Dinan, 2005; Dunning, 1997; Ehlermann, 1987) and, in consequence, this market's rules guarantee free movement of goods, services, capital and people. These four free movements are the essence of our empirical analysis when assessing the impact of Brexit on the EU-28. There are at least four different scenarios for designing new UK-EU relations (Chalmers, 2016; Ebell & Warren, 2016; Fossum, 2016; House of Commons, 2013; House of Commons Foreign Affairs Committee, 2013):

- the Norwegian option, known as the EEA model, which means an admission to the EEA with all the consequences;
- the Swiss option, which would result in signing dozens of bilateral agreements negotiated between the UK and the EU;
- the Turkish option, which means the creation of a custom union between the UK and the EU; and
- the WTO option, which means using the WTO's most-favored-nation (MFN) principle to arrange trade relations between the UK and the EU.

In practice, the arrangement could be a hybrid of the four different options, depending on the results of the long and complex negotiation process. Therefore, we hypothesize that:

> H6: The more EEA-like the perceived solution for the future UK-EU relations, the greater the companies' engagement in the UK.

Some economists perceive Brexit as a unique opportunity for the British economy to increase its growth rate and competitiveness (Minford, Gupta, Le, Mahambare, & Xu, 2015; Minford, 2017). According to the World Bank, companies bear less tax burden in the UK than in many other European countries even now, with the UK still in the Common Market. Companies are not forced to pay territorial economic contribution (CET) and spend significantly less on social security contributions (Boone & Kuhanathan, 2016). If we add to that a relatively high labor market efficiency and technological readiness, the British market stands out as a good destination for FDIs. If the future UK–EU relations would not encourage capital flows, the British government might be tempted to uphold the existing corporate policies or even enforce more favorable policies (Hestermeyer & Ortino, 2016). Now, the number of Polish-originating companies established in the British market exceeds 40,000 and keeps growing. Therefore, the potential restrictions imposed on trade arrangements may sway the companies toward equity investments. Therefore, we hypothesize that:

> H7: The relatively more favorable economic policy instruments in the UK compared to other countries, the greater the companies' engagement in the UK.

Compared to other EU countries, on average, Poland does not trade much outside of the Common Market. Polish companies are four times more focused on the European market than on other markets. Should Polish companies choose non-European destinations, there prevail the United States, China and Canada. One of the reasons for the situation at hand may be the low structural competitiveness of Polish exports, increasing costs to export to geographically distant locations, the relative lack of experience, and – as statistical data shows – low Polish-originating MNEs contribution. SMEs tend to turn to locations without trade barriers that simplify the transaction process, often choosing the Common Market over external destinations (Bergami, 2017). However, as the future relations with the UK will most probably entail significant restrictions, the companies may be forced to seek demand elsewhere (Rickard, 2015). Bearing in mind the fact that other EU-27 countries cannot accommodate the additional surplus – not only from Poland but possibly from other countries turning back from the UK – the companies may search outside of the Common Market (Langan, 2016). Therefore, we hypothesize that:

> H8: The higher the expected increase in the number of trade opportunities outside the EU, the lower the companies' engagement in the UK.

The currency exchange rate is influenced by a set of fundamental and technical factors. As one of those factors, Brexit has definitely had its toll on currency exchange rates in the recent months. The forecasted amplitude of changes varies depending on the adopted scenario. Since the British referendum, the pound has been on the decline because of both the voting results and the political developments that followed. As for the Polish zloty, it is not only the PLN/GBP rate that is in question (Belke & Gros, 2017). The exchange rates of other currencies are perfectly correlated with the uncertainty caused by Brexit. According to Statistics Poland, the value of Polish exports significantly exceeds the value of imports, meaning that the companies dependent on the UK's market fear the loss of potential income (Swati, Ottaviano, & Sampson, 2017). Furthermore, the uncertainty when – and whether at all – the exchange rate rebounds may cause the companies to seek alternative, more stable markets. Hence, we hypothesize that:

H9: The greater the increase in volatility of the GBP/PLN exchange rate, the lower the companies' engagement in the UK.

What determined companies' presence in the UK in the pre-Brexit period of 2017–2019? Results of the study

Table 7.9 presents the operationalization of variables used for testing the hypotheses. Since data were obtained with the use of the same method – questionnaires – we checked for common method bias. The variance inflation factors (VIF) in no case exceeded the 3.3 threshold (Kock, 2015), which indicated that the strength of the relationships between the variables was not overstated. Since VIFs were less than 10, we also encounter no multicollinearity problem.

Table 7.9 Variables operationalization

Dependent variable	Symbol	Operationalization	VIF
Company's engagement on the British market	Y1	Share of sales in the UK in total sales	–
Change in company's engagement on the British market	Y2	A 5-point scale measure indicating how companies changed their involvement in the British market between 2017 and 2019 (1 – significant drop in involvement; 5 – significant increase in involvement)	–
Independent variable	*Symbol*	*Explanation*	*VIF*
Ties with the UK	X1	The share of sales in the UK in the total foreign sales and share of a company's imports from the UK Cronbach's alpha: 0.88	1.266
Diversification of geographical destinations	X2	The number of locations (regions) the company made sales (1–6)	1.257
Entry modes	X3	A 3-point scale measure indicating 1 – only non-equity entries, 2 – only equity entries, 3 – both equity and non-equity entries	1.510
Demand	X4	A 5-point scale measure indicating how companies considered the demand to influence their strategy in the British market (1 – very negative influence; 5 – very positive influence) Assessment of demand in • Poland • UK • Other countries	1.239
	X5		1.699
	X6		1.306

Dependent variable	Symbol	Operationalization	VIF
Intensity of rivalry	X7	A 5-point scale measure indicating how companies considered the intensity of rivalry to influence their strategy in the British market (1 – very negative influence; 5 – very positive influence)	1.560
	X8		1.871
		Assessment of rivalry in	
		• Poland	
		• UK	
Form of economic relations	X9	A 5-point scale measure indicating how companies considered the difference between adopting the EEA-like scenario and the "no deal" scenario (1 – change in scenario has no impact; 5 – change in scenario has a very strong impact)	1.431
The UK's corporate policies	X10	A 5-point scale measure indicating how companies considered economic policy in the UK toward foreign companies to influence their strategy in the British market (1 – very negative influence; 5 – very positive influence)	1.464
Currency exchange rate	X11	A 5-point scale measure indicating how companies considered the changes in the currency exchange rate to influence their strategy in the British market (1 – very negative influence; 5 – very positive influence)	1.800
Relations with external partners	X12	A 5-point scale measure indicating to what degree companies sought partners outside the EU (1 – did not engage in a search at all; 5 – very strongly engaged in a search)	1.087
Control variable	Symbol	Explanation	VIF
Industry	X13	Dummy variable indicating if a company belongs to the production or non-production industry	1.318
Company size	X14	Turnover	1.515
	X15	Number of employees	1.909
Company's experience	X16	Number of years dealing with sales in the British market	1.306
Capital group	X17	Dummy variable indicating if a company belongs to a capital group or not (0–1)	1.471

Source: Own elaboration.

The correlation analysis did not indicate a problem with dependent-variable collinearity except for six pairs of variables (Table 7.10). The choice of entry modes was positively correlated with turnover and capital group membership, which was to be expected since companies' decisions about entry mode typically depend on ownership structure and company size. The intensity of rivalry in Poland and in the UK are also correlated, which is justified, as it is normally dependent on the industry characteristics such as industry concentration and entry barriers. Furthermore, these two factors correlate with the perception of

Table 7.10 Correlation matrix

	Y1	Y2	X1	X2	X3	X4	X5	X6	X7	X8	X9	X10	X11	X12	X13	X14	X15	X16	X17
Y1	1.00																		
Y2	–	1.00																	
X1	0.56	−0.15	1.00																
X2	−0.04	0.19	−0.33	1.00															
X3	0.08	0.65	−0.26	0.25	1.00														
X4	−0.07	−0.08	−0.11	0.01	0.05	1.00													
X5	−0.09	0.00	−0.08	0.00	0.03	0.16	1.00												
X6	−0.13	−0.06	−0.14	0.01	0.02	0.24	0.27	1.00											
X7	−0.16	−0.12	0.10	−0.13	−0.21	0.07	0.16	0.00	1.00										
X8	−0.10	−0.13	0.13	−0.19	−0.19	0.02	0.22	0.05	0.45	1.00									
X9	−0.15	−0.03	−0.06	−0.01	−0.03	0.14	0.24	0.13	0.18	0.30	1.00								
X10	−0.09	−0.04	0.20	−0.18	−0.21	−0.06	0.10	−0.05	0.40	0.42	0.15	1.00							
X11	−0.13	0.00	−0.11	−0.10	0.00	0.15	0.37	0.28	0.18	0.27	0.33	0.14	1.00						
X12	0.01	−0.06	0.07	−0.09	−0.10	−0.13	−0.18	−0.15	0.02	0.08	0.01	0.07	−0.12	1.00					
X13	0.16	0.15	−0.35	0.31	0.24	0.02	0.01	0.04	−0.28	−0.28	−0.10	−0.28	−0.08	−0.09	1.00				
X14	0.14	0.24	−0.19	0.19	0.50	0.05	−0.01	0.05	−0.26	−0.24	−0.03	−0.25	−0.05	−0.04	0.18	1.00			
X15	0.15	0.30	−0.27	0.19	0.42	0.02	0.03	0.05	−0.21	−0.14	−0.01	−0.21	0.01	0.01	0.24	0.73	1.00		
X16	0.12	0.09	−0.29	0.22	0.26	0.03	0.10	0.03	−0.20	−0.10	0.03	−0.23	0.10	−0.01	0.38	0.32	0.35	1.00	
X17	0.12	0.35	−0.21	0.26	0.42	−0.07	−0.01	−0.01	−0.15	−0.08	−0.01	−0.11	−0.04	−0.09	0.38	0.16	0.25	0.27	1.00

Source: Own elaboration.

British corporate policies toward foreign companies. Again, this dependence does not raise objections as all three variables concern the bigger issue of competitive factors influencing company strategies in the British market. Finally, the two control variables describing company size correlated very strongly: turnover and the number of employees. We initially considered excluding one of them from the analysis but – since VIFs did not point to any problems – we eventually included both control variables into the model.

The F-test value suggests that we deal with a significant linear regression. The R2- and R2-adjusted for model 1 are 57% and 55%, respectively, while for model 2 are 46% and 44%. On the one hand, this suggests that the models do not fully explain the degree of company changes in their engagement in the British market while, on the other hand, the models are high enough in comparison to other studies in the IB field. The Durbin-Watson test was close to 2 (1.93 and 2.03 for models 1 and 2, respectively), which suggests no issue with autocorrelation in residuals. Table 7.11 presents the regression results.

First, we analyzed hypotheses H1–H3, which are related to the company's internationalization degree. We found that there is strong evidence to suggest that

Table 7.11 Regression model estimations

	Degree of engagement				Changes in engagement			
	Beta	*Standard error*	*t(482)*	*p*	*Beta*	*Standard error*	*t(482)*	*p*
Constant	−6.00*	3.64	−1.65	0.10	2.79***	0.21	13.05	0.00
X1	40.62***	1.84	22.11	0.00	−0.05	0.11	−0.48	0.63
X2	0.50	0.44	1.14	0.26	0.00	0.03	−0.09	0.93
X3	−0.11	0.30	−0.37	0.71	0.26***	0.02	14.80	0.00
X4	0.12	0.48	0.26	0.80	0.08**	0.03	2.67	0.01
X5	−0.28	0.49	−0.57	0.57	−0.04*	0.02	−1.55	0.10
X6	−0.36	0.49	−0.74	0.46	−0.04*	0.02	−1.57	0.10
X7	−0.83*	0.47	−1.57	0.10	0.02	0.03	0.54	0.59
X8	−0.17	0.47	−0.35	0.72	−0.04	0.03	−1.33	0.19
X9	−0.75**	0.38	−1.97	0.05	0.02	0.02	0.80	0.42
X10	−0.12	0.40	−0.29	0.78	0.04*	0.02	1.89	0.06
X11	0.45	0.42	1.07	0.28	0.00	0.02	−0.16	0.87
X12	0.18	0.25	0.73	0.46	0.02*	0.01	1.72	0.10
X13	4.87***	0.67	7.27	0.00	0.00	0.04	0.09	0.93
X14	0.28	0.52	0.55	0.59	0.00***	0.15	0.88	0.00
X15	0.00	0.00	0.94	0.35	0.03**	−0.18	0.85	0.03
X16	0.30***	0.05	5.71	0.00	−0.01*	0.00*	−1.76	0.08
X17	3.14***	0.86	3.62	0.00	0.12**	0.05	2.36	0.02

Source: Own elaboration.

***$p < 0.001$; **$p < 0.5$; *$p < 0.10$.

companies with previously established strong economic relations with the UK were prone to have a higher engagement in that market in years 2017–2019. However, this factor did not impact their decisions on whether to change the degree of their engagement. Therefore, hypothesis H1 is partially supported. However, we found no support for hypotheses H2, which suggested that the more geographically dispersed the company's operations, the less likely it would uphold its British operations. The model indicates that no statistically significant relationship between company's engagement – or changes in that engagement – in the British market and the company's geographical scope was to be found. Hypothesis H3 suggested that the company's engagement would be dependent on the entry mode. We found that the degree of engagement was not impacted by entry mode at all, but the changes in that degree were. If companies used equity modes or a combination of equity and non-equity modes, they were more likely to uphold or even increase their presence in the British market. One of the control variables – a company's experience in the British market – also proved significant in both models. The longer the company has operated in the British market, the more engaged it was in this market. However, as far as changes in this engagement are concerned, the beta value was close to 0, which means that it scarcely impacts the relationship.

Next, we turned to factors that related to industry's pressure. Hypothesis H4 suggested that company's engagement in the UK was dependent on the demand the company experienced in various markets. The degree of engagement revealed no statistical dependence on demand factors, but the changes in that degree did reveal such a dependence. As we assumed, the higher the demand in the UK and the lower in other countries, the more willing the companies were to uphold their engagement in the British market. However, once again, the beta value was not high, suggesting that the dependence was not strong. In hypothesis H5, we assumed that the engagement would also be influenced by the level of rivalry in the industry. However, in both models, these factors proved statistically insignificant, hence giving no support to our assumptions.

Finally, we analyzed the development of the UK-EU relations and their impact on the company's presence in the UK. Hypothesis H6 suggested that company strategies would be impacted by the fear (or its lack) over the future arrangement of relations between the UK and EU. This factor was reported as highly significant in the model concerning the degree of company's engagement in the UK. The higher the fear over the form of relations, the lower the company's engagement. Hypothesis H7 concerned the perception of UK's policy and corporate regulations toward foreign investors. This factor emerged as significant in relation to changes in the degree of company's engagement in the British market. The better the policies were perceived, the more likely companies were to uphold their activities in the UK. Furthermore, we verified how the perception of exchange rate fluctuations impacted the company strategies. It turns out that exchange rate had no real effect on company strategies in the discussed period. Finally, we verified whether companies also considered the possibility of exploring new non-EU markets to substitute the UK's withdrawal. This factor proved to be significant in terms of changes in the company's engagement in the UK. Surprisingly, the companies that turned to new ventures were also keen on upholding their activities in the British market. That unexpected outcome corresponds with the types of strategies we distinguished among the companies (for more, see Chapter 8).

Conclusions

Although there are many potential factors that could influence company behavior in the pre-Brexit period, the group of determinants is not as wide as we assumed. Companies do fear Brexit as the process is seen as a game changer but, in most cases, their strategies are not overly impacted by the potential policy changes. As far as their degree of engagement in the British market is concerned, the companies mostly fear the possible developments of the future regulations between the UK and the EU. The question on how these factors matter varies as well, depending on whether we consider the actual degree of engagement or the changes that appeared in this engagement in 2017–2019. Regardless, it does seem that these two years have not brought significant changes to companies' attitude toward the British market. It remains to be seen whether the actual Brexit and – especially – the post-transition period will bring significant changes to the meaning of these factors.

References

Anderson, E., & Gatignon, H. (1986). Modes of foreign entry: A transaction cost analysis and propositions. *Journal of International Business Studies, 17*(3), 1–26. https://doi.org/10.1057/palgrave.jibs.8490432

Belke, A., & Gros, D. (2017). The economic impact of Brexit: Evidence from modelling free trade agreements. *Atlantic Economic Journal, 45*(3), 317–331. https://doi.org/10.1007/s11293-017-9553-7

Bergami, R. (2017). Brexit: Australian perspectives on international trade and customs operations. *Australian & New Zealand Journal of European Studies, 9*(1), 2–14. Retrieved from https://esaanz.org.au/wp-content/uploads/2017/11/1-Brexit-Australian-Perspectives-on-International-Trade-and-Customs-Operations.pdf

Boone, L., & Kuhanathan, A. (2016). Brexit the French way: Regulation, tax, and politics. In Ch. Wyplosz (Ed.), *What to do with the UK? EU perspectives on Brexit* (pp. 37–44). London: CEPR Press.

Brouthers, K. D. (2002). Institutional, cultural and transaction cost influences on entry mode choice and performance. *Journal of International Business Studies, 33*(2), 203–221. https://doi.org/10.1057/palgrave.jibs.8491013

Chalmers, D. (2016). Alternatives to EU membership and the rational imagination. *The Political Quarterly, 87*(2), 269–279. https://doi.org/10.1111/1467-923X.12259

Cyert, R., & March, J. (1992). *The behavioral theory of the firm.* Hoboken, NJ: Wiley-Blackwell.

Dinan, D. (2005). *Ever closer union: An introduction to European integration.* Boulder, CO: Lynne Rienner Publishers.

Dunning, J. H. (1997). The European internal market programme and inbound foreign direct investment. *Journal of Common Market Studies, 35*(2), 189–223. https://doi.org/10.1111/j.1468-5965.1996.tb00593.x

Ebell, M., & Warren, J. (2016). The long-term economic impact of leaving the EU. *National Institute Economic Review, 236*(1), 121–138. https://doi.org/10.1177/002795011623600115

Ehlermann, C. D. (1987). The internal market following the single European act. *Common Market Law Review, 24*(361), 361–409.

Fossum, J. E. (2016). Norwegian reflections on Brexit. *The Political Quarterly, 87*(3), 343–347. https://doi.org/10.1111/1467-923X.12287

Hestermeyer, H., & Ortino, F. (2016). Towards a UK trade policy Post-Brexit: The beginning of a complex journey. *King's Law Journal, 27*(3), 452–462. https://doi.org/10.1080/09615768.2016.1254416

House of Commons. (2013). *Leaving the EU.* Research Paper, No. 13/42. Retrieved from www.parliament.uk/briefing-papers/RP13-42/leaving-the-eu.

House of Commons Foreign Affairs Committee. (2013). *The future of the European union: UK government policy.* Retrieved from www.publications.parliament.uk/pa/cm201314/cmselect/cmfaff/87/87.pdf

Kock, N. (2015). Common method bias in PLS-SEM: A full collinearity assessment approach. *International Journal of e-Collaboration, 11*(4), 1–10. https://doi.org/10.4018/ijec.2015100101

Langan, M. (2016). Brexit and trade ties between Europe and commonwealth states in sub-Saharan Africa: Opportunities for pro-poor growth or a further entrenchment of North – South Inequalities? *Round Table, 105*(5), 477–487. https://doi.org/10.1080/00358533.2016.1233758

Lazowski, A. (2012). Withdrawal for the European Union and alternatives to membership. *European Law Review, 37*(5), 523–540.

Minford, P. (2017). From project fear to project prosperity, an introduction. *Economists for Free Trade.* Retrieved from www.economistsforfreetrade.com/wp-content/uploads/2017/08/From-Project-Fear-to-Project-Prosperity-An-Introduction-15-Aug-17-2.pdf

Minford, P., Gupta, S., Le, V. P. M., Mahambare, V., & Xu, Y. (2015). *Should Britain leave the EU? An economic analysis of a troubled relationship.* Cheltenham: Edward Elgar.

Mullainathan, S., & Thaler, R. H. (2000). *Behavioral economics.* NBER Working Paper, no. 7948, National Bureau of Economic Research. https://doi.org/10.3386/w7948

NBP. (2016). *Foreign direct investment (inflows) in Poland.* Retrieved from www.nbp.pl

Nicolaides, P. (2013). Withdrawal from the European Union: A typology of effects. *Maastricht Journal of European and Comparative Law, 20*(2), 209–219. https://doi.org/10.1177/1023263X1302000204

Nicolaides, P., & Roy, T. (2017). Brexit and trade: Between facts and irrelevance. *Intereconomics/Review of European Economic Policy, 52*(2), 100–106. https://doi.org/10.1007/s10272-017-0654-y

Porter, M. E. (1980). *Competitive strategy.* New York: Free Press.

Porter, M. E. (2008). The five competitive forces that shape strategy. *Harvard Business Review, 88*(1), 78–93.

Radner, R. (1996). Bounded rationality, indeterminacy, and the theory of the firm. *The Economic Journal, 106*(438), 1360–1373. https://doi.org/10.2307/2235528

Rickard, S. (2015). Brexit: Ultimately it's trade that matters. *International Journal of Agricultural Management, 5*(1/2), 1–3. https://doi.org/10.22004/ag.econ.262383

Simon, H. A. (1972). Theories of bounded rationality. In C. B. McGuire & R. Radner (Eds.), *Decision and organization.* Amsterdam: North-Holland Publishing Company.

Sorensen, J. O. (1997). *The internationalisation of companies: Different perspectives of how companies internationalize.* Aalborg: International Business Economics Working Paper Series.

Swati, D., Ottaviano, G., & Sampson, T. (2017). A hitch-hiker's guide to post-Brexit trade negotiations: Options and principles. *Oxford Review of Economic Policy, 33*, 22–30. https://doi.org/10.1093/oxrep/grx005

Williamson, O. E. (1985). *The economic institutions of capitalism: Firms, markets, relational contracting.* New York: Free Press.

8 Strategies of Polish companies against Brexit

Results of the empirical study

Barbara Jankowska, Aleksandra Kania,
Katarzyna Mroczek-Dąbrowska

Introduction

The UK's withdrawal from the EU will have significant repercussions for citizens and companies across Europe. With its four freedoms of goods, services, labor and capital, the European Common Market provides a level playing field, replacing 28 sets of regulations with a single rule book and free access to 500 million customers for companies. After Brexit, the UK is likely to lose full access to the single market, making it a less attractive destination for companies looking to use it as a base for their EU investments. European companies exporting to the UK will also have to rethink their strategies.

For some countries, such as Germany, it remains important to preserve the logic of the European project; for others, such as Poland, it is essential to preserve its citizens' ability to freely move and work across Europe. However, we should not overlook the fact that appropriate Brexit strategies are not only developed at the macro level but also at the micro level. We observe that entrepreneurs from various EU countries react differently to this new situation of exceptional complexity and unprecedented nature.

Even though Germany as a country will most probably not be severely impacted by Brexit (PricewaterhouseCoopers, 2016), German entrepreneurs remain apprehensive. As mentioned in Chapter 3, according to the research done by the Association of German Chambers of Industry and Commerce (Deutsche Industrie- und Handelskammern, 2018), German companies plan to move their investments mainly to the home market of the other EU-27 member states. About half of the companies consider relocating their investments to Germany, another EU country, Switzerland or Norway, and a third of them consider their future destination to lie outside Europe.

According to current projections, also the Polish economy will mostly probably not suffer from substantial consequences (e.g., Borowski, Olipra, & Błaszyński, 2018). However, Brexit will still introduce many changes for Polish companies. Considering the Polish context, we may assume that Brexit will be particularly damaging for two groups of companies as follows:

• Companies that, so far, have dealt only with trade in the single market and, therefore, are unfamiliar with non-standard procedures. They are often SMEs.

- Companies with internationalized and complex production chains that must export and import semi-finished products multiple times before their final product is finished, which often requires a customs declaration each time.

There are many possible ways in which Polish companies can adapt to this situation of ever-growing uncertainty. In this chapter, we try to establish a detailed typology of different strategies that Polish entrepreneurs are undertaking in the face of Brexit, even though its final shape and form has not been determined yet.

Company strategy in foreign markets: the Ansoff Matrix

In order to study the Polish companies' response to Brexit and identify types of strategies Polish entities develop to address the deep and difficult change, we need first to refer to an existing typology of corporate strategy. The literature in the field of strategic management provides many diverse approaches to describe corporate strategy. Nevertheless, the classic approach that often works as the foundation for the more modern and recent typologies of corporate strategies is the Igor Ansoff's Matrix, first published in 1957 in *Harvard Business Review* (Ansoff, 1957; Nagji & Tuff, 2012). This typology of corporate strategies is universal, which means that it can be applied by companies from different industries, with diverse internationalization ambitions, be it public or private entities.

The Ansoff's approach is called a product-market matrix because it refers to the two following criteria: either an existing or a new product and either an existing or a new market (Figure 8.1). Combining these two dimensions of product and market, we may distinguish four basic types of strategies:

- market penetration;
- product development;
- market development; and
- diversification.

Each type of this strategy must be translated to specific actions on the side of a company.

Even though this approach is quite old, executives and managers continuously employ it to identify the strategies their businesses may follow. The Ansoff Matrix helps to notice which strategies may be riskier and which represent a less demanding option. The least risky strategy is the market penetration while the riskiest is the diversification strategy.

In the market penetration strategy, enterprises focus on increasing their sales in existing markets, which translates into market share growth in these markets. Companies that pursue this strategy often acquire a competitor in their market of operations and use marketing-mix instruments to lure more clients, i.e.,

Figure 8.1 The Ansoff's Matrix adaptation

Source: Own elaboration based on Ansoff (1995).

they reduce prices to attract new customers or invest more in promotion and distribution efforts.

The product development strategy means that a company aims to offer new products in its current markets. Thus, the company prioritizes the development of its product portfolio, which calls for much research and development efforts and investment in innovations. This strategy may be useful for companies that understand their present markets and want to accept the risk of innovation. Companies may conduct R&D operations within their own organizations or decide for partnership with competitors to develop a new product together.

The third option is market development that manifests itself in entering new markets with existing products. The term "new market" may be interpreted in many ways: entering a new geographical region within its home market, entering a new country which means company internationalization or entering a new customers segment. Market development is the right course of action when a company is in charge of a proprietary technology that it can exploit in new markets and when potential clients in new markets do not differ too much from the existing ones.

Finally, there is the diversification strategy, which focuses on entering a new market with new products. Firms may pursue related and unrelated diversification. The first option is less risky. Diversification provides the company with the best growth potential. Companies may achieve greater revenues but must accept greater higher risk.

Companies' approach to Brexit

Between the vote on Brexit and the final date of the UK leaving the EU, companies were granted almost four years to readjust their strategies. Still, although Brexit is a done deal, we are unsure about the exact regulations that would govern the UK–EU relations afterward. Therefore, based on the sample of 500 Polish companies that established business relations with the UK market before the Brexit vote (for sample details, see Chapter 7), we analyzed the types of strategies adopted by firms when they were still unsure of the shape of Brexit.

We applied the k-means grouping method to verify how company strategies differed. Our analysis was focused on market-penetration, i.e., we identified company strategies from the sales perspective and not from the sourcing perspective. In our analyses, we included the following factors:

- F1: the increase in scale (intensity) of business relations with the UK;
- F2: the increase in scale (intensity) of business relations in the domestic or already acquired markets;
- F3: search for new potential markets to enter within the EU;
- F4: search for new potential markets to enter outside the EU;
- F5: the abandonment (or major decrease in scale) of the UK market;
- F6: the development of new products/services in the British market; and
- F7: the development new products/services and their introduction to other, already acquired markets.

All the above factors were measured with the use of a 5-point Likert scale, in which 1 stood for refraining from such actions and 5 stood for applying them on a large scale. After the initial analysis, we concluded that factors F5 (UK's market abandonment) and F6 (developing new products/services in the British market) were not significant in delimiting company strategies. These two activities were applied to a minor degree, so we did not include them in the final list of grouping factors. Accordingly, for the remaining factors we have conducted the variance analysis to verify whether they were a good fit for grouping purposes (Table 8.1).

The *F*-value is high enough for all factors to be concluded as significantly differentiating strategy types. This means that our results fulfilled the goal of minimizing the within–cluster variance and maximizing the between-cluster variance. Next, with the aid of the Ward's method, we established the appropriate number of strategy types that we wanted to identify. We intended to build on the four-pole Ansoff Matrix, so we have verified whether that would be the

Table 8.1 Results of the variance analysis

Factor	Between cluster	df	Within clusters	df	F -value	Significance p
F1	269.5284	3	226.6637	496	196.5998	0.00
F2	142.8241	3	304.1259	496	77.6441	0.00
F3	181.2066	3	245.1214	496	122.2231	0.00
F4	253.4273	3	404.2447	496	103.6500	0.00
F7	331.4482	3	87.3518	496	627.3419	0.00

Source: Own elaboration based on survey reports.

Strategies of Polish companies against Brexit 125

appropriate number of clusters. Since dendrograms confirmed that four groups would indeed be sufficient, we then based our analysis on four pre-determined groups. The k-means grouping analysis obtained results after three iterations (Table 8.2).

Based on the mean values (Table 8.3), we identified four types of strategies companies adopted in the pre-Brexit period:

- Strategy 1: *Observers* were companies that took no action at all;
- Strategy 2: *Cautious expanders* were companies still offering their core activities but searching to expand on alternative, relatively known (EU) markets;
- Strategy 3: *Opportunity seekers* were companies seeking to penetrate the British market but also to find alternative markets to expand to with their current portfolio; and
- Strategy 4: *Diversifiers* were companies searching for new sales opportunities worldwide but simultaneously expanding their portfolio.

Table 8.2 Group mean values

Factor	Strategy 1	Strategy 2	Strategy 3	Strategy 4
F1	1.66	1.76	3.69	1.86
F2	1.62	2.65	2.73	3.36
F3	1.95	3.50	3.51	3.40
F4	1.43	2.70	3.28	3.61
F5	1.17	1.04	1.24	3.27

Source: Own elaboration based on survey reports.

Table 8.3 Characteristics of companies undertaking different pre-Brexit strategies

Feature	Observers	Cautious expanders	Opportunity seekers	Diversifiers
Number of companies in the sample	95	230	90	85
Company size	No size pattern	Small- and medium-size companies	No size pattern	Small- and medium-size companies
Dominant industries	Production	Non-production	Production	Non-production
Average company age	25 years	23 years	24 years	20 years
Ownership structure	Mix of Polish-owned and foreign-owned companies	Polish-owned companies	Mix of Polish-owned and foreign-owned companies	Mix of Polish-owned and foreign-owned companies

(*Continued*)

Table 8.3 (Continued)

Feature	Observers	Cautious expanders	Opportunity seekers	Diversifiers
Average experience in the British market	17 years	14 years	16 years	14 years
Average revenues from the UK (%)	12.5	11.5	14	11.5
Dominant entry mode	Direct and indirect exports	Direct and indirect exports	Joint venture	Direct exports

Source: Own elaboration based on survey reports.

These strategies clearly stem from the Ansoff Matrix and the decision on whether to penetrate the British market, seek alternative markets or launch activities in new industries; or, a combination of each of them. Therefore, Figure 8.2 presents the *pre-Brexit strategies* compared to commonly known development strategies in the Ansoff Matrix.

Let us note that some strategies adopted by companies duplicate the exact Ansoff strategies, i.e., diversifiers launch new activities that expand beyond their core businesses and simultaneously seek new markets for these activities, while cautious expanders seek new markets that could substitute the British market once the Brexit enter with full force. However, two other strategies – namely observers and opportunity seekers – emerged as hybrid solutions. In truth, observers take no action at all, upholding the relationship with the British market but without strengthening it either. On the other hand, opportunity seekers intended to strengthen their activities in the UK while, at the same time, they search for alternative markets to safeguard their revenues in the case of abrupt deterioration in trade regulations. Of course, the adopted strategies were characteristic to a specific type of companies (Table 8.4).

Some characteristics – like the average company age, experience in the British market and revenues in the UK – were relatively similar among all the studied companies, while other differed. SMEs dominated among cautious expanders and diversifiers, but there was no exact size pattern among observers and opportunity seekers. As for industry breakdown, observers and opportunity seekers included mainly production companies while cautious expanders and diversifiers – non-production companies. As for the dominant entry mode in the British market, most strategies referred to exporting companies, but opportunity seekers were dominated by firms that formed joint ventures. We may conclude that cautious expanders' and diversifiers' strategies were popular among the similar type of companies (e.g., by size, industry, age or ownership) while observers' and opportunity seekers' strategies were targeted by yet another, also similar group.

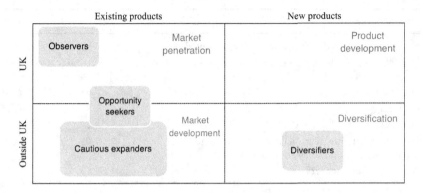

Figure 8.2 Pre-Brexit strategies in comparison to Ansoff's matrix

Source: Own elaboration.

Table 8.4 Extent of company's withdrawal from the British market by type of strategy

Strategy	Withdrawal from the British market				Domain limitation				Activity scale limitation			
	Observers	*Cautious expanders*	*Opportunity seekers*	*Diversifiers*	*Observers*	*Cautious expanders*	*Opportunity seekers*	*Diversifiers*	*Observers*	*Cautious expanders*	*Opportunity seekers*	*Diversifiers*
Applied	1%	5%	1%	0%	1%	11%	5%	5%	4%	13%	5%	5%
Not applied	99%	95%	99%	100%	99%	89%	95%	95%	96%	87%	95%	95%

Source: Own elaboration based on survey reports.

Although almost none the companies reported to overall withdraw or significantly downsize their involvement in the British market, firms have nevertheless limited their activities in specific company operations (Table 8.5). Strategy that involved most reductions in the British market were implemented by cautious expanders: ca. 5% of the companies withdrew from the British market, ca. 11% limited the number of industries they were involved with and ca. 13% downsized the scale of their involvement in that market. Among other types of strategies, the number of companies that declared such steps was even smaller, in general reaching less than 5% of the sampled companies.

Based on the Kruskal-Wallis test, we specify in Table 8.6 which areas of company's functioning in the British market differed in each type of the identified strategy. The results indicate which functions were differently approached by different strategies and not whether they were downsized or not. More details on the scope of their limitation can be found in Figure 8.3.

Table 8.5 Kruskal-Wallis test results on downsizing activities

Strategy feature	H	P
Which activities of the company have been limited or liquidated in the British market		
Production	2.38	0.50
Distribution	*10.98*	*0.01*
Logistics	*7.85*	*0.05*
Research and development	*38.27*	*0.00*
Supporting activities (e.g., accounting, human resource management, promotional activities, etc.)	*14.02*	*0.00*
After-sales customer service	5.10	0.16

Source: Own elaboration based on survey reports.

Note: Italics are statistical significant.

Table 8.6 Kruskal-Wallis test results on competitive strategy

Changes in competitive strategy	H	p
From cost leadership to product/service differentiation	1.20	0.75
From product/service differentiation to cost leadership	5.00	0.17
No change – remained with cost leadership strategy	*15.00*	*0.00*
No change – remained with product/service differentiation strategy	*14.99*	*0.00*

Source: Own elaboration based on survey reports.

Note: Italics are statistical significant.

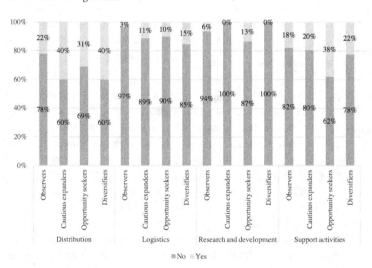

Figure 8.3 Withdrawal or downsizing of company's activities in the British market by strategy type

Source: Own elaboration.

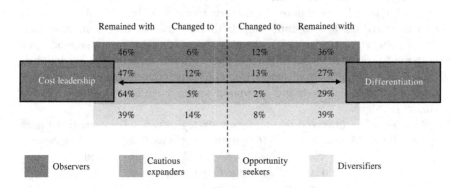

Figure 8.4 Changes in competitive strategies amongst studied companies

Source: Own elaboration.

The results of the Kruskal-Wallis test indicate that significant differences were noted in distribution, logistics, R&D and supporting activities performed in the UK market: the significance level in each case was lower than 0.05. Therefore, in Figure 8.3, we specify how frequently companies reached for such solutions in each strategy type.

Regardless of the strategy type, if changes were indeed implemented, most downsizing activities occurred in distribution and support activities. Cautious expanders and diversifiers limited their scope of sales activities by as much as 40%. In support activities, these were the opportunity seekers who cut their involvement in the British market to the highest degree: by 38%.

It is important not only to discuss whether companies were willing to uphold their activities in the British market but also to analyze how their competitive strategies changed in the pre-Brexit period. Again, based on the Kruskal-Wallis test, we verified whether there were significant changes among the identified strategies. We studied four possible options that emerged from Porter's division: changes between cost leadership and differentiation or the upholding of one of those strategies.

Based on the analysis of our results, we noted that significant changes were visible among the companies that remained with their original competitive strategies in the British market. As Figure 8.4 indicates, there were no drastic differences between strategies adopted in each of the identified types. Cost leadership dominated slightly in comparison to differentiation mode, but only among opportunity seekers it exceeded 70%. Otherwise, the division was relatively equable.

Summary

Based on the data from survey reports, we divided Polish companies into four groups: *observers, cautious expanders, opportunity seekers* and *diversifiers*. We divided them by considering such factors as the intensity of business relations with the UK, the intensity of business relations in the domestic or already acquired markets, search for new potential markets to enter within the EU, search for new potential markets to enter outside the EU and the development of new products/services in acquired markets. We found that the groups coincide well with the Ansoff Matrix. We found that *diversifiers* and *cautious expanders* duplicate exact Ansoff strategies of diversification and market development, whereas two other strategies – *observers* and *opportunity seekers* – are hybrids of the existing Ansoff strategies.

Moreover, we observed that company strategies were characteristic of their specific types. Most companies (46%) in the sample were usually *cautious expanders*. They could be characterized as SMEs, specializing in non-production activities, 23 years old, with the average experience in the British market of 14 years. Their average revenues from that market reached 11.5% and were mostly coming from indirect and direct exports. The second biggest group (18%) were *observers*, who shared a similar profile. However, most companies from that group specialized in production activities.

Furthermore, we compared company strategies with potential competitive strategies designed by Porter – cost leadership and differentiation – to find that there were no drastic changes in strategies among the identified types of studied companies. In this chapter, we presented various strategies of Polish companies undertaken in the face of Brexit in the last couple of years. Predicting a more distant future of Polish companies in Europe after Brexit remains a difficult and delicate task.

References

Ansoff, I. (1957). Strategies for diversification. *Harvard Business Review, 35*(5), 113–124.

Ansoff, I. (1995). *Corporate strategy: An analytical approach to business policy for growth and expansion.* New York: McGraw-Hill.

Borowski, J., Olipra, J., & Błaszyński, P. (2018). The impact of hard Brexit on Polish exports. *International Journal of Management and Economics, 54*(2), 99–109. https://doi.org/10.2478/ijme-2018-0010

Deutsche Industrie- und Handelskammern. (2018). *The impact of Brexit on German businesses.* Retrieved from www.ihk-nuernberg.de/de/media/PDF/en/dihk-impact-of-brexit.pdf

Nagji, B., & Tuff, G. (2012). A simple tool you need to manage innovation. *Harvard Business Review, 5,* 2–12.

PricewaterhouseCoopers. (2016). *Leaving the EU: Implications for the UK economy.* Retrieved from www.pwc.co.uk/economic-services/assets/leaving-the-eu-implications-for-the-uk-economy.pdf

9 Strategies of Polish companies against Brexit

Case studies

Barbara Jankowska, Aleksandra Kania,
Piotr Trąpczyński

Introduction

Amica: Polish manufacturer of household appliances ventures to the UK

Amica S.A. is a Polish manufacturer of kitchen appliances. The company was founded in 1945 and since then has developed its international profile. Nowadays, Amica is the largest Polish manufacturer of household appliances and one of the most recognized companies listed on the Warsaw stock exchange. Amica belongs to those original equipment manufacturers (OEMs) and end–user companies with a majority of Polish capital. It is a part of a group of large private firms with more than 250 employees listed on the stock exchange. Almost 70% of its sales is generated in export markets, while 30% on the domestic market. Amica sells its products under different brand names, depending on the region. Its strategy is based on building strong regional brands that are recognizable in the given country. Amica aims to become one of the top three cooking appliance producers in Europe with a planned sales revenue of EUR 1.2 billion by 2023.

Amica's history

Amica's first gas/coal cooker was produced in Wronki in 1957. Amica's appliances, produced in Wronki, are now very well known throughout the European markets. Over 50% of the company's production is currently exported, and its plans for the next few years are expected to generate further growth in export sales. The first step undertaken by Amica S.A. was export to Germany in 1960s. Company's global expansion on a bigger scale has begun since its privatization in 1994, with first acquisitions in the early 2000s.

Amica's international expansion started with help of the owner's previous experience in exporting (Figure 9.1). Foundation for the future development of export was laid by the German firm that joined the group with the owner. Then the Polish economy underwent dramatic changes that made increased internationalization possible for the local companies. In the early 2000s, Amica bought a Scandinavian refrigerator company with a strong, well-recognized

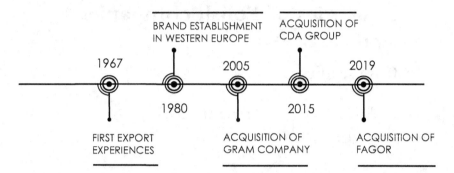

Figure 9.1 History of Amica's international development

Source: Own elaboration.

brand. As a next step Amica started to develop its presence in Russia and on the Eastern European markets through their German brand.

"*It was all hit and miss in the beginning*" – says Alina Jankowska – Brzoska, Vice President Sales and Marketing at Amica. "We started with exporting and we still export a lot of products to the Balkans, Post-Soviet countries, Vietnam, Thailand, Israel, Australia etc. At some point however we developed our strategy and started acquiring companies on different European markets. It's much easier to distribute our products through distribution channels already developed by the acquired firms. Our latest acquisitions include a British and a French company. The British firm produces and designs studios for kitchen furniture under its own brand – CDA. The French company doesn't have its own brand and adjustment of its business model to ours was a difficult task" (Jankowska-Brzoska, 2020, September 11).

Amica plans to increase its global presence in the future. This strategy stems from the growing saturation of the European markets and increased competition from Chinese players, which are acquiring new companies in a very fast pace. The company plans to stick to its international expansion model in the future: a mix of export and acquisitions, depending on the geographical distance and country's political and cultural conditions.

Nowadays, the Amica Group generates more than 70% of its revenue from sales on over 70 global markets. The company is most popular in Germany, Great Britain and Scandinavia. Its subsidiaries are located in Denmark, Germany, England, Spain, France, Russia, Ukraine, China and Romania. Nevertheless, the company sells its products also in other regions of the world, such as Asia or the Middle East. Amica respects the peculiarities of foreign markets. For example, in the UK, over 30 brands can be found competing with one another. Whereas, the customers on the German market have high-quality expectations and are very loyal to their German brands and the Amica brand is not known well. Both markets need to be approached with a different strategy. Bearing in mind different profiles of particular foreign markets, Amica Group portfolio includes three international brands:

- Gram, which was established in 1899 and acquired by Amica in 2005, is a traditional and prestigious Denmark-based brand known throughout Scandinavia.
- Hansa, which is a brand associated with reliable technology, is very popular on the Eastern European markets.
- CDA, a British brand acquired in 2015, enjoys superb recognition in such distribution channels as design studios for kitchen furniture.

The group employs approximately 2,500 people at its plants and offices in Poland and abroad.

Amica is keen on innovation and it contributes to its competitive advantage. The innovative solutions have been implemented inside the company and are broadly used to lure clients. In the set of the technologies that contribute to its strength belongs: cloud computing, big data, mobile technologies and social media. To effectively exploit these solutions Amica's employees broadly use the digital equipment – computers, smartphones, tablets and take advantage from the Internet and Intranet (Götz & Jankowska, 2020). The company has been trying to follow the pace of the Industry 4.0 and implements the Industry 4.0 solutions within the customer support systems (CRMs), enterprise resource planning (ERP), manufacturing execution systems (MESs) and energy management systems (EMSs). Next to the mentioned big data analytics and cloud computing, Amica uses autonomous robots, horizontal and vertical system integration, exploits the Industrial Internet of Things and respects much the cybersecurity solutions. The firm's involvement in the Industry 4.0 contributes to the cost reductions and reduction of time necessary to perform particular processes. The Industry 4.0 technologies are used to better develop new products. Thus, the cost advantage plays a role but at the same time the differentiation attitude is quite visible in Amica's approach toward the market.

The challenge of Brexit is accompanied by the challenges related to the Industry 4.0, thus the effective strategy to cope with Brexit is partially conditioned by the firm's ability to adjust to the new technological landscape. It calls for the reconstruction of the employment and organization of dedicated trainings to upgrade the automation competencies in manufacturing and investment in cybersecurity solutions not forgetting about the constant need for research and development focused on new products. This is an issue as Amica operates in industries with short product life cycles. Evident manifestation of Amica's attempts to face the challenges of the changing technological landscape that simultaneously enables the company to better cope with the Brexit turbulences is the opening in 2017 of the high-bay warehouse in Wronki, Poland (Mika, 2017). The company invested in that approximately PLN 57 million. Those days it was the tallest high-bay warehouse in Poland and one of the tallest in Europe. It can store 230,000 large household appliances. The warehouse has an automated steering system capable of processing about 1.6 thousand new items per hour. This innovative solution upgrades Amica's advantage since its products reach its customers at least a day earlier, and its entire stock is placed in a single place. Bearing in mind the strong internationalization of the company the new warehouse optimizes its logistics costs. Thanks to that, Amica may better serve its customers not only in Poland but abroad, in UK among others.

Amica's activity on the British market in face of Brexit

The Amica Group began working with British partners in 2009. At the time of Brexit referendum, the UK was not among the three foreign markets generating the highest sales revenues for Amica. These were France, Germany, Russia and the share of sales revenues generated in the British market in total sales revenues reached 8.7% in 2017–2019.

The company's preparations for Brexit started in the beginning of 2019. At that time, the Risk Department conducted a risk analysis with the assumption of hard Brexit. This was the moment when British companies began to fear problems with Chinese supply chains. The punctuality of transports was questionable. The need to complete additional formalities at customs points was also taken into account. For this reason, the Amica Group decided to increase the level of inventories. It was necessary to rent an additional warehouse at a price 30–40% higher than the current market prices. It can be said after the fact, that it was not the right decision, from the financial point of view. Action was taken too late; as rental prices had risen drastically. The high level of inventories was maintained for a year and the costs of this venture were very high. This action could have had a positive effect in the event of a hard Brexit, but from a 2020 point of view, it was not effective and cost the group £0.5 million. In this context, it can be concluded that pre-emptive action, if there is a risk of significant cost increases, is inappropriate. Additionally, the situation was complicated by the COVID-19 pandemic. In the beginning of 2020, CDA had high inventory but limited sales opportunities. When sales increased in the second half of the year and inventories were sold out, problems with the supply chain appeared, including redirection of containers to the United States from China, which generated long delays in deliveries. Trust in the CDA brand is largely based on timely deliveries and situations in which the goods together with the furniture do not reach the customer on time pose a significant threat to the company's image. Table 9.1 presents short- and long-term threats to CDA in connection to Brexit on January 1, 2021.

One of the possible advantages for the company after Brexit may be the availability of a larger pool of specialists on the labor market, who would be inclined to move to Nottingham and work with a slightly less competitive salary than before. The availability of specialists may result from the fact that some foreign economic entities have left the British market, which may result in an increase in the supply of the labor factor. Currently, the lack of skilled labor is a serious problem. Low availability of such staff is related to the location of the company

Table 9.1 Short- and long-term perspective threats to CDA

Problematic field	Interpretation
Short-term perspective	
Logistics problems	There will be new transport procedures, customs issues, institution preparation, etc. that will have to be worked out
Additional costs	One of the examples refers to the use of SAP system by CDA. SAP servers are set up in Poland and the question is how it will work after Brexit. The group must consider the costs of transferring the data to the UK
Legal issues	The company has to take into account the problem of regulating the form of employment of Polish workers in the CDA and their possible movement between Poland and Great Britain
Long-term perspective	
Consumer purchasing power in the UK	The company will most probably face a decline in UK consumer purchasing power due to the rising unemployment
Decline in company's competitiveness	Most of the company's competitors produce in Europe and CDA's supply chain relies heavily on China. If import duties from China to the UK are higher than import duties from EU to the UK, all CDA's goods will become less competitive by default
Absence of final agreement with EU as of January 1, 2021	The company also fears political instability and chaos in case of absence of final agreement with EU as of January 1, 2021

Source: Own elaboration.

employing about 150–200 people in a small town. The group is also consider-ing moving the company to a larger agglomeration (in the vicinity), in face of lower rental prices after Brexit. A more attractive location could encourage more qualified specialists to work at CDA.

At the moment, the Amica Group is not planning to change its strategy in face of the upcoming Brexit. Although it seriously considers the methods of financing its activities and, as a commercial company, decides to finance locally – in Poland, without cooperating with entities from the UK. The company consistently builds its image on the British market, paying particular attention to the employee's identification with the company. This is evidenced by the use of the CDA logo, the dress code of employees and the colors of the trucks that transport the company's products. The high inventory levels in 2019 and the resulting additional costs discouraged the company from taking preventive measures. Nevertheless, in the fourth quarter of 2020, Amica plans to re-analyze the risks. CDA customers in Great Britain are currently waiting for the actions of producers and importers and awaiting actions of the British government. Competitors, to the company's knowledge, also do not take any additional adaptive and preventive measures. The British market, or rather the group of the company's clients, is very fragmented and at the same time very demanding. Kitchen stores cooperating with the company do not maintain stock levels, which requires Amica to be extremely efficient in terms of product deliveries. The high bargaining power of customers on the British market turns out to be an even greater challenge in reference to the current COVID-19 pandemic.

Aztec International – multinational player adapting to the British market

Aztec International S.A., headquartered in Poland, is a European capital group and a cooperating partner of American Aztec Washer Inc. group based in California. The Poznań-based MNE is a leading European supplier of a broad spectrum of powder painted screws, Master Seal washers, Master Flash roof/pipe flashings and Master Plug fastening systems, as well as anchors and rivets. The production unit specializes in powder painting a different type of fasteners. For these purposes, an own-designed technology and Master Coat machinery, developed and manufactured by Aztec. The products of the company products could be found in roughly 25 markets.

Aztec International is known for its reliability, usage of high-quality raw materials and superior powder painting service, as well as short-order processing times and quick delivery to any location within Europe. The existing production capacity allows Aztec International to paint more than 1 million screws daily, while continuous quality control during the manufacturing process as well as directly before the shipment to clients help ensure high standards of the delivered products.

While being controlled by foreign individual shareholders, the Aztec International enjoys a high degree of autonomy, whereby the Poznań-based management team is responsible for an ongoing surveillance of the European operations, as well as corporate growth from a strategic perspective. Thus, Aztec International is not a subsidiary of a foreign company and enjoys substantial decision autonomy, while being able to benefit from the know-how of sister companies controlled by the same US-based investors. Accordingly, with regard to product and process innovation, Aztec International draws from the know-how of the associated companies Aztec Washer Company (Poway, CA, USA) and Aztec Nordic Ltd Oy Ab (Tammisaari, Finland). This focus on quality helps the company stand out in a market dominated by mainstream products produced in locations characterized by lower labor costs, which aim at price-sensitive clients, particularly those based in emerging markets.

The group is listed at the New Connect stock exchange in Poland. In 2019, Aztec International attained revenues at the level of PLN 25.97 million, an increase of 26.8% over the preceding year (Aztec International, 2020). At the same time, the net result amounted to roughly PLN 0.45 million, a decrease of about 76.7%.

Aztec's history

In August 2001, Aztec Polska Sp. z o.o. was established, with headquarters in a small town of Kaźmierz Wlkp. The start-up launched its first machine for powder painting and assembling in November of the same year. This capacity was already doubled thanks to new machinery in July 2002. In July 2003, Marek Ciulis joined the company as official procurator. In the same year, with continuous growth of the company, the headquarters was moved to the major regional city of Poznań. In 2004, the launch of the third painting and assembling machinery took place. In May 2007, the change of the company name to Aztec International occurred. At the same time, leadership of the company was taken over by Marek Ciulis who was appointed Chief Executive Officer. The management change also coincided with a significant enhancement of the company's production capacity, which now rose to the level of up to 1,000,000 screws daily owing to the start-up's fourth substantial investment in machinery.

In order to accommodate for the company's development, in August 2008, the company status was changed and it was transformed into a joint-stock company. The company was re-named to Aztec International S.A., so as to reflect its increasing internationalization degree and growing responsibility for managing foreign markets. To support the rising complexity of the organization, an integrated management informatics system CDN XL was implemented in January 2009. At the external communication level, it was crucial for the ambitious company to build up its reputation with a view to targeting the most demanding European clients. With that in mind, the company obtained the European Technical Approval for farmer screws in April 2010. In order to further enhance its innovative capacity, Aztec International invested in a state-of-the-art saddle washer painting machine in June 2010. A month later, the company's official debut on the stock exchange in Warsaw took place.

With new financing in place, the company embarked a period of intensive international expansion, which continued without major changes until the Brexit and the COVID-19 pandemic shook international markets. The company signed its biggest trade agreement in its history with a building materials distributor which is present in international markets in July 2011. In August 2011, a milestone in the international growth of the firm was achieved: the acquisitions of two building companies from the UK and from Germany were completed. In January 2012, the Supervisory Board appointed Rafał Cędrowski as the Vice-President of the Management Board, thereby integrating a value-based approach into the international management of Aztec's operations. Aztec International kept pursuing trade agreements with distribution partners and direct clients, with major deals struck back in January and September 2012. The further development of the firm's international activities will be discussed in the ensuing sections below.

Aztec International's international strategy

Aztec International's international operations began in 2008. Since then, the company managed to introduce its products in about 25 markets, of which Finland, the UK and Germany are the most important ones in terms of revenue. This fixing systems manufacturer generated on average more than 95% of its sales from foreign markets in the period 2017–2019. It can be regarded as a predominantly Western Europe-focused firm, which is also a consequence of the international outlook of the management team. As mentioned in the preceding sections, the international capital group cooperates with contractual associates, i.e., external firms (in such countries as Finland or Mexico) providing technological solutions exclusively to Aztec International. Therefore, from the viewpoint of the management team, the technological and, consequently, product-related superiority poses an important competitive advantage in developed countries. While the firm regards the development of business relationships in Western Europe as more complex and time-consuming, it also recognizes that such approach is more beneficial for the overall competitiveness of the firm in the long run, as compared to engaging in quicker, but also rather temporary, price-driven transactions in less developed markets of Central and Eastern Europe. Indeed, as Rafał Cędrowski, the Chief Financial Officer of Aztec International noted, "*it is price that matters the most in these markets, customers are ready to sacrifice quality to obtain a high discount*" (Cędrowski, 2020, October 21). As Polish firms find themselves positioned between competitors from both the least developed and – consequently – the cheapest locations, and on the other hand firms from the most technologically advanced economies, thus not necessarily being able to compete exclusively on pricing. On the contrary, these products need to be good enough to compete on par with those from Western producers. As the CFO of Aztec International observed, putting an emphasis on Eastern, less saturated markets would mean a short-term orientation in international expansion, as the seemingly quick, lower-margin business transactions in less saturated market conditions provide only "*short-lived advantage, which leaves such firms in financial trouble after 3–5 years*". In fact, operating in less demanding markets does not incentivize companies to improve their products and services, while business partners may show lower reliability in terms of paying their liabilities. Aztec International's long-term approach to developing international markets requires continuous investments in maintaining superior product quality, as well as state-of-the-art service level and competitive conditions.

Aztec International's activity in the UK in the context of the Brexit

Aztec International's activity in the British market dates back to 2008 when export sales began. The group then acquired a local company with established market position in 2011. While the company operates in most foreign markets through independent distributors, a more direct commitment to the British market was mainly related to a better exploitation of its significant potential, which would be limited due to geographic distance. In that context, given the transport costs and the emphasis on product quality, service level and delivery times, the possession of locally based operations was of strategic relevance. Moreover, as the CFO underlined, *"the British market is specific from our perspective . . . The adaptation of products requires having local operations to a larger extent than in other markets in which we have been present"*.

The UK subsidiary was gradually restructured and enhanced, in terms of scale and scope of activities. Since 2013, production has been opened in the UK, as well, with a new technological line. While this decision did not enable operational synergies with the Polish parent firm due to substantial geographic distance, it is instrumental to a more efficient way of serving of the British market. The British subsidiary was also supplied with technological know-how from cooperating R&D units in Finland and the United States, enabling the British company to enhance the technological edge of the whole offering. The British quality control department further helps to ensure that the Aztec brand stands out among competitors. The local presence is also important from the perspective of building up business relationships and developing trust with local partners. Also, the ability to tap into local talent was among important motives to invest in wholly owned operations in the UK.

The result of the Brexit referendum in the UK came in as a surprise to many foreign firms operating in that market. From the point of view of Aztec International, the potentially uncertain future development could be a substantial challenge to the realization of its international strategy given the relevance of the British market. The previous consequent enhancement of British operations was based on the premise of adapting to the highly competitive market, shortening the supply chain and serving the local market demand at satisfactory margins. However, in order to streamline the overall international operations of the group in an efficient manner, the company was planning to consolidate product supplies from the Polish manufacturing unit and warehouses to European sales markets, including the UK. The start of the Brexit process meant a challenge to that more centralized approach from several perspectives.

Firstly, a stronger reliance on transports from continental Europe would mean more exposure to potentially higher customs fees, as well as less favorable VAT settlement rules. Moreover, as the consolidated business model for European markets assumed obtaining standardized product certifications broadly recognized in continental Europe, the lack of mutual recognition of product quality norms and permissions would entail additional investment in products tests and application for new certifications for the UK market. Therefore, from the perspective of the management team of Aztec International, the most serious threat would be a Brexit without a deal with the EU, as well as the increase of tariff and non-tariff-related barriers to trade with Great Britain. Moreover, the company regarded the overall political instability in the UK as a factor affecting business planning in a particularly negative way (see Table 9.2).

Table 9.2 Aztec International's assessment of Brexit impacts on UK operations

Brexit-related factors	Impact
Costs related to customs	Moderately negative
Cost of passport right loss	Neutral
Cost of VAT settlement	Neutral
Cost of permits for service delivery and product import	Moderately negative
Transport costs	Moderately negative
UK's economic policy in 2017–2019	Highly negative
Expected shape of relations with the UK based on Common Market principles	Moderately negative
Expected shape of relations with the UK based on customs union	Moderately negative
Expected shape of relations with the UK based on WTO rules	Moderately negative
UK's exit without a deal with the EU	Highly negative
GBP to PLN exchange rate in the period 2017–2019	Neutral
Expected increase in tariff barriers in the trade with the UK	Highly negative
Expected increase in NTBs in the trade with the UK after the Brexit	Highly negative
Political instability in the UK	Highly negative
Public trust in politicians and public administration and their approach to foreign firms in the UK	Moderately negative
Competencies and efficiency of British administration in the period 2017–2019	Moderately negative

Source: Own elaboration.

In order to minimize the operational and financial impacts of the Brexit, the planned modifications in the European business model were abandoned, with a view of maintaining the autonomy of the British subsidiary. While the group was striving at operational synergies across different country markets, the possible barriers to international business with the UK required to assume a self-sustainable model for the British operations. Thus, the local manufacturing and warehousing capability of the subsidiary was sustained. Moreover, the company remains committed to developing new products for the British market and keep its upmarket positioning, evading price-based competition on the part of low-cost products. From a broader perspective, the diversified portfolio of export markets of Aztec International provides an additional level of immunity to Brexit's impacts. In fact, the group can compensate temporary fluctuations in a given market with sales performance in higher-performing markets and provide within-group financial and operational support to the subsidiary in need. While this is not directly a Brexit-induced strategy, Aztec International's diversification acts as a buffer in a period of uncertainty.

Aztec International belongs to internationally operating, Polish capital groups which can be regarded as relatively well prepared for different Brexit scenarios and well positioned to reduce the potential financial and operational impacts of the entire situation on its functioning. The company boasts a significant internationalization degree in terms of foreign revenues and the number of served international markets; therefore, it can offset local hindrances with performance in other markets. Moreover, the start of the Brexit process and the uncertainty surrounding it sparked off internal strategic discussion within the group, which reinforced the strategic autonomy of the British subsidiary in order to make it prepared for the most negative post-Brexit scenario and reduce exposure to different risk factors.

References

Aztec International. (2020). *Skonsolidowane sprawozdanie finansowe za rok obrotowy od 1 stycznia do 31 grudnia 2019 roku (Consolidated financial statement 1st January 2019–31st December 2019)*. Retrieved from https://newconnect.pl/ebi/files/119282-3.-roczne-skonsolidowane-sprawozdanie-finansowe-sig-sig-sig.pdf

Cędrowski, R. (2020, October 21). Personal Interview.

Götz, M., & Jankowska, B. (2020). Adoption of industry 4.0 technologies and company competitiveness: Case studies from a post-transition economy. *Foresight and STI Governance*, 14(4), 61–78. https://doi.org/10.17323/2500-2597.2020.4.61.78

Jankowska-Brzoska, A. (2020, September 11). Personal Interview.

Mika, T. (2017). *Amica has launched its own warehouse*. Retrieved from https://warehousefinder.pl/blog/news/amica-has-launched-its-own-warehouse

10 The new normal

Brexit and the EU

Marian Gorynia, Barbara Jankowska,
Katarzyna Mroczek-Dąbrowska

Introduction

In accordance to the Withdrawal Agreement, the UK left the structures of the EU on January 31, 2020. The UK is now officially a third party that neither participates in the decision-making process of the EU nor does it follow its dictate. However, not much has changed as the EU law still applies in the UK and citizens as well as businesses both in the UK and in the EU did not have to "change their ways". And so, it will continue till the end of the transition period. The businesses and we – the society – are kept in a political, legal and regulatory vacuum. With no certainty can we expect that the Political Declaration promising facilitations in trade, movement and investment will be met. The expected changes concern amongst others: taxation, customs, export/import licensing and VAT. Therefore, the European Commission along with the British authorities urge companies to act and adopt before the transition period expires.

One cannot say for certain, how long it will take companies to adapt – companies report that they expect to change within 9–15 months since the moment the new order is introduced. However, some companies, either out of precaution or facing the challenge ahead, have already strategized their existence in the British market. As the studies show, companies are not willing to give up the British market – they do not disinvest and neither do their significantly decrease their involvement in trade. That only shows that despite Brexit the relationship remains strong. But at the same time, businesses diversify. Companies seek new markets that will make up for the potential loss in the UK both in the EU and outside it.

The book's focus

Taking into account the importance of the UK in foreign trade relations with the EU, the question of future cooperation is crucial for companies. Uncertainty about the shape of this relations increased, given the mixed economic signals observed in the last years – depreciation of the pound and reduction of the interest rates in the UK and at the same time higher than assumed growth and foreign trade (increase in UK's trade deficit – imports higher than exports).

Hence, it becomes increasingly important to study whether Brexit has and will have a significant influence on companies' business strategies. Companies were frequently studied in reference to strengthening and facilitating the regional integration and thus deepening their expansion. The reverse situation, when firms are forced to cope with the uncertainty of disintegration process can add to the understanding of the theory of the firm and strategic planning. Notably very little has been written to what extend companies do take into consideration macroeconomic forecasts and whether they adopt a reactive or proactive approach (cf. Keen, 2017).

The microeconomic perspective on the Brexit focusing on its impact on the companies' strategies is of utmost importance for the EU and the Central-European countries that have tight economic relations with the UK. By most Brexit is seen as an inconvenience if not a threat (Hertner & Daniel, 2017; Springford & Tilford, 2014) and therefore requires adaptive moves. At the same time, companies do not suffer from and respond to the change in the same way. There is hardly any research on the company's strategies toward Brexit. One of the reasons for that is the limited data availability. Information on approaches toward Brexit cannot be found in any official statistical data and requires in-depth analysis at the core of the setting – the company. This on the other hand requires time and other resources. This volume aims to understand different approaches undertaken toward the UK's exit and to understand its meaning for the whole economy.

The volume's highlights

The volume is directly related to various disciplines in broad fields of economics and management: microeconomics and macroeconomics, the theory of the firm, industrial economics, strategic management and international business, public economics and economics of law. Since the main focus of the research is set on a company and its future approach toward foreign markets, the main assumptions refer to both the theory of the firm and the strategic management. The subject discussed concerns the company's international activities and as such relates to international business. Given the uncertainty surrounding the Brexit, it is probable that some of the industries are bound to be more influenced than the other, and so the book also relates to industrial economics.

As the topic of Brexit is vital, publications on Brexit are numerous. However, this volume distinguishes itself with the focus set on company perspective. Businesses are imminent to the changes caused by the UK's withdrawal, and in many cases, their survival in this market is set by their adaptive capabilities. In this way, this book calls for rethinking their company strategies, so that the hardship of the "divorce" can be minimized. Although companies do not directly influence the policymaking, their early responses to the prepared regulations guide the negotiations and alter the negotiating edge.

The chapters included in this volume offer a complex narrative on Brexit consequences to the EU member states and particularly to businesses. EU has for long been the model example for regional integration and thus the disruption caused by Brexit undermines the very idea of integrating. The migration issue, the struggle for power, budget allocations and trade-off between national interests and reaching consensus have tarnished the UE's segue to full integration. Yet, the observed struggle to uphold the UK-EU relationship strong indicates that the topic of Brexit's business impact is an important addition to the unfolding debate of the EU's future (cf. Bulmer & Quaglia, 2020).

Brexit is a fact but its long-lasting effect is not yet known. The volume looks ahead to where we – as society but first and foremost as economies – find ourselves on the adaptivity curve. Predicting what comes next calls to mind fortunetelling but at the same time waiting unprepared for whatever unfolds is asking for failure. The challenge is set as we cannot say for certain that Brexit is the one and only disruption to come.

The book's content and audience

Recent developments on international political scene, pushed the UK in spotlight as the process itself poses significant international effect. And yet very few observers would be able to point to and explain factors and mechanisms behind these processes. By shedding light on the latter and most importantly trying to indicate strategies to embrace Brexit, this volume constitutes a substantial contribution to the debate. Importantly, in this way, it adds to several related debates pertaining to: how motives of internationalization in developed countries change in time; what conditions need to be met for companies to uphold their international engagement in a country when faced with abrupt and unsupportive changes; how the uncertainty and information asymmetry impact on the company's decision-making process. The book should be of particular interest to scholars, undergraduate and graduate students across diverse fields of study, inclusive of International Business Studies, Strategic Management, Politics, European Studies, Public Policy, Economics as well as International Political Economy.

Brexit: toward the new normal

It has become a common practice, to call events that occur completely unexpectedly as black swans – these are very unlikely events, but they bring significant losses. Likewise, the white swans are the events of which existence we know and which are not of great surprise (cf. Aven, 2014). In this respect, 2020 is quite unusual. Along many events and processes taking place worldwide – and to which we have already gotten used to – we have encountered one black swan of considerable size and great importance. Quite few white swans of international reach such as the US confrontation with Iran, cyber war, declining US-China trade relations, US presidential elections, costs of climate change and – last but not least Brexit – are now accompanied by one black swan – the COVID-19 pandemic.

One of the aforementioned white swans is Brexit. Before becoming white, for some time it was recognized as a black one – the occurrence of which, in principle, no one expected or assumed. It was a theoretical, formally admissible, but so unimaginable event that in reality it was not considered as a realistic option. The initial attitude toward Brexit can only be described as completely dismissive. And yet this swan which appeared so suddenly, quickly settled in society's mind as well as in the political and public sphere. After the Brexit referendum, the black swan turned into a white one – it was no longer surprising, we got used to its notion with only its timing and policy regulations remaining uncertain.

With the COVID-19 pandemic under way, many question whether we still should bother with Brexit and its outcome. But we do. The pandemic has without doubt changed the business reality and the "new normal" will – for long to come – not be the normal we have gotten used to. But still, the radical plunge in the economy (and especially in certain industries), along with volatility of labor market and reshaping of the business models is yet more amplified with the Brexit uncertainty. We face the world of two uncertainties – one we can hardly control but the other we can and should mold to our liking.

The COVID-19 pandemic seems to have a multidimensional impact on Brexit both for the countries directly involved, and for the European and global economy. The pandemic certainly distracts the attention of political decision makers and public opinion from the UK's withdrawal from the EU, which on the one hand may delay the political process and on the other hand may mitigate potential conflicts between the interested parties (i.e., the EU and the UK) due to the "oversaturation" of the events.

In June 2020, Michael Gove, the representative of Great Britain in the negotiations between the EU and the UK announced that there would be no extension of the so-called transitional period, i.e., a period in which the UK is not formally but de facto still remains a member of the Union. The UK left the Community after January 31, but although its rights are severely limited, it still has to comply with EU law and enjoys the rules of the Common Market (cf. Trommer, 2017). Paradoxically, it seems that the COVID-19 pandemic will seal a quick divorce between the EU and Great Britain, as British politicians see it as a good opportunity to implement the "Get Brexit done" election slogan. It also seems increasingly possible to return to the so-called hard Brexit scenario, i.e., parting without a contract. The negative effects of such a solution overlap with the problems caused by the pandemic, so that no one will be able to distinguish one from the other.

References

Aven, T. (2014). *Risk, surprises and Black Swans. Fundamental ideas and concepts in risk assessment and risk management.* London & New York: Routledge.

Bulmer, S., & Quaglia, L. (2020). *The politics and economics of Brexit.* London & New York: Routledge.

Hertner, I., & Daniel, K. (2017). Europhiles or eurosceptics? Comparing the European policies of the labour party and the Liberal Democrats. *British Politics, 12*(1), 63–89. https://doi.org/10.1057/bp.2016.4

Keen, S. (2017). Trade and the gains from diversity: Why economists failed to predict the consequences of Brexit. *Globalizations, 14*(6), 803–809. https://doi.org/10.1080/14747731.2017.1345104

Springford, J., & Tilford, S. (2014). *The Great British trade-off.* Centre for European Reform. Retrieved from www.cer.org.uk/sites/default/files/publications/attachments/pdf/2014/pb_britishtrade_16jan14-8285.pdf

Trommer, S. (2017). Post-Brexit trade policy autonomy as pyrrhic victory: Being a middle power in a contested trade regime. *Globalizations, 14*(6), 810–819. https://doi.org/10.1080/14747731.2017.1330986

Index

Note: Page numbers in *italics* indicate a figure and page numbers in **bold** indicate a table on the corresponding page.

Printed in the United States
by Baker & Taylor Publisher Services